THE BOOK OF

FLORIDA FISHING

By Gordon Lewis

Illustrated by

Rube Allyn

WITH A FOREWORD BY DR. F. G. WALTON SMITH, DIRECTOR,
UNIVERSITY OF MIAMI MARINE LABORATORY

GREAT OUTDOORS
PUBLISHING CO.

4747 TWENTY-EIGHTH STREET NORTH ST. PETERSBURG, FLORIDA 33714

TO MY FATHER

A splendid sportsman who taught me the art of the cast, the thrilling anticipation of the strike, the beauty of waters and open spaces, and the serenity that settles on the soul of man pursuing the fine sport of angling.

International Standard Book No.: 0-8200-0102-3
Library of Congress Catalog Card No.: 56-11379

REPRINTED:
June 1971, Dec. 1972, Jan. 1974, Feb. 1975, Nov. 1976, Oct. 1978
June 1979, Feb. 1981, Sept. 1981, Aug. 1982

Printed by Great Outdoors Publishing Company

Manufactured in the United States of America

FOREWORD

The angler new to Florida, or wishing to extend his fishing to new areas of the state, will naturally welcome this really informative fishing guide with its detailed presentation of Florida sports fishes. He will find firsthand information on identification, the feeding habits, likely localities, preferred lures, and methods of catch.

Many fishing guides, handbooks, and aids to identification of Florida fishes hitherto available have fallen into two classifications. There were those written by the ichthyologists that were designed more for the scientist than the angler, more concerned with scientific names and technicalities than with the practical questions the angler seeks to answer. Others, regional guides limited in scope, too often appear to be compilations of material extracted from earlier publications, judging by the way in which old errors have been passed from one to the other. Mr. Lewis' book is refreshing to read and use, since it falls into neither category.

The angler needs the kind of practical information that comes both from careful research and from firsthand information, and Mr. Lewis is well qualified to provide it. He has not based this book exclusively on earlier printed sources but has drawn on his own careful observations, and, as a result, fishermen will find in it just what they are looking for.

The arrangement itself is also commendable, since it allows the reader to locate what he seeks quickly and without looking up ichthyological family groupings. He will be glad to learn the most likely places for finding his favorite fish rather than be confronted with the usual "distribution" information which gives undue prominence to the location of rare stragglers.

In fact, once the angler makes the acquaintance of *The Book of Florida Fishing,* he is likely to make it as much a part of his angling gear as his tackle.

DR. F. G. WALTON SMITH
Director, University of Miami
Marine Laboratory

CONTENTS

Author's Note

The Book of Florida Fishing is a book conceived with the idea of providing for the average fisherman and the newcomer to Florida a practical aid in identifying and knowing the fish he is most likely to encounter, basic information about their location and habits, and the most widely accepted methods of catching them.

The work is not intended for the ichthyologist, the scientist, or the advanced fishing "purist"—people to whom this writer, however, is indebted for much of the information popularized within. Nor is it for that pleasant school of advanced anglers who spend hours debating fine points of species, habits, seasonal color variations, and controversial determinations of scientific names which have little use for practical angling purposes.

There are many excellent books available that detail in scholarly completeness all the saltwater fish of the nation. The Book of Florida Fishing confines itself to Florida. Every recognized principal game fish has been included, following the Standard Check List of Principal Salt Water Game Fishes compiled by the Outdoor Writers' Association of America, and the names accredited by the American Society of Fishes. The principal freshwater fishes of Florida are equally thoroughly dealt with.

Identification has been designed to give sharp and distinctive descriptions that will permit the angler to know the fish he is catching and liable to catch. In the matter of names, it is hoped the reader will be pleased that four, six, or as many as ten synonymous names have not been used to designate any one fish (a procedure interesting to the student of fish, but one that may well be confusing to the angler who has not made exhaustive studies).

Here the common, accredited name of the species is given, followed by the scientific name, and then the one or two names by which the fish is most popularly known in Florida. The usual—in this matter of names, as well as in habits, feed and methods—is always given consideration over the unusual, and the intricacies of some species' variations omitted as of no importance to the fisherman who wants to enjoy himself catching fish in the sunny waters of Florida.

It is further hoped the reader will find this cutting through to essentials a helpful, easy guide in learning about the fish of Florida. Much of the value of the book, beyond its accuracy—achieved both as a result of intensive research through authoritative publications and the writer's long years of experience in Florida—lies in its organization.

It will be quickly noted that the fish appear in alphabetical order. This should permit an easy reference by thumb. At the same time, a consistent pattern has been followed to allow the reader to determine at a glance under the headings name, scientific name, common Florida name, identification, location, methods of fishing, habits, edibility, and weights, the exact information about any particular fish he wishes to know, without reading through several pages that lump all the information together.

The book has been designed, aimed, and written for the people who eagerly look to fishing as a healthful pastime, a wonderful sport, a pleasurable part of life that takes them to open spaces for thrilling experiences in the warming sun and colorful waters. It is hoped it will prove to be an interesting aid in the pursuance of their sport.

*The Wonderful World of Florida Salt-Water Sports Fishing**

The mighty tarpon knows no limits to his aerial acrobatics. Power, versatility, and magnificent courage combine to give the flashing silver king first place as the most admired of Florida's numerous great game fish.

Florida stands unique in the minds of fishermen the nation over — those who already know its translucent waters and those who dream of the day they will.

It is unique in its vast, varied coastlines (the longest of any state in the Union), unique in its fish-filled waters that offer a myriad of salt-water game species so easily accessible to anglers in all walks of life—fish to be caught by methods of the individual's choosing while moving about in pleasant, soothing temperatures, and surroundings of sub-tropical beauty.

In the early days of sports fishing, enthusiastic fish and game writers beat the drums for the fish of Florida, a little uncertainly, perhaps, but with a gusto and fervor equal to that of the thousands of angler-writers who followed them with a seemingly inexhaustible fund of stories, articles and books on Florida fishing lore.

C. S. Clarke, writing in FOREST AND STREAM, the earlier name for the venerable FIELD AND STREAM, warned his readers in 1876 that, if they were considering a trip to the jungles and wilderness of Florida, to "beware of a great and dangerous fish known to natives as the 'tarpum'. This fish," he continued, "is said to attain a size of 100 pounds, so savage it can be killed only with a harpoon. A fisherman seeing tarpum should remove his bait from the water to keep his tackle from being destroyed."

But the immediate humor of this fades when you consider the gear of those days—the cumbersome, non-multiplying reels, the heavy, uncertain rods, the unevenly made lines. A trip to Florida was in the nature of a safari if you planned to go south of St. Augustine on the East Coast, or by boat to Key West or Tampa. It was necessary to purchase your outfit for the most part in the larger cities of the North. Once you had hired guides to take you up the St. Johns—the river that flows north—or down the great inland bay of the Indian River, and a "tarpum" or two had made off with your lines and rods, broken a thumb, or spilled you out of the boat with an unceremonious leap to the seat alongside you, your fishing for that particular long trek was finished.

Even in the year 1956 there are anglers who will heartily agree that the tarpon is a "savage"

*Some portions of this have appeared in *Sports Illustrated* and *True,* to whom thanks are extended for their permission to reprint it here.

fish and a threat even to the finely perfected tackle of modern times. Not a year passes in Florida which does not produce tall stories of the antics of the mighty silver-sided fighter of the shallower waters, only to be displaced by a still more fabulous tale the next day or the next month.

The modern approach to fishing in Florida is a matter of individual choice, tempered only by restrictions of time and money. There are the great game fish of the Gulf Stream, for which one must employ a guide and a charter-boat if one does not have a large craft suitable for offshore waters, with the proper tackle specifically designed for heavy duty. These include sailfish, blue and white marlins, mako shark, tunas, wahoo, the big amberjack of the reefs, and schools of kingfish which flow up the Florida coasts during their migration period. The mighty tarpon are hunted in shore waters, flats and bays, and bonefish and permit are sought on the flats. Seatrout fishermen in many portions of the state pursue their special quarry, as do devotees of redfish, snook and pompano.

Then there are the bottom fish, the grab bag of the reefs and bays, river mouths and mangrove-banked islands and keys. These fish, incredibly varied in size, shape and species, take the whole range of baits offered by fishermen. This exciting lottery begins its play every time a line enters the water. The unexpected becomes the expected after a while—the barracuda, rushing a snapper lure (or a snapper itself), oversize grouper, striking while one is trolling for big barracuda, a stray cobia, taken while one is bridge-fishing a channel for crevalle jack, a tarpon, which might pick up a piece of cut mullet which was aimed at grouper. This is the kind of excitement, the fast change of pace, the encounter with the unusual that make angling in Florida salt waters the ever-varied, dramatic and eternally interesting sport that it is.

Fish populations overlap everywhere in Florida's salt water, but to the veteran fisherman who, rod in hand, has gradually worked his way throughout the state, a certain pattern of the fish, and the best methods of catching them which are particular to certain areas in certain seasons begin to take shape.

The northernmost part of the East Coast of Florida was once quickly passed up by sports fishermen in a hurry to reach the Palm Beaches, Miami or the well-known Gulf spots. As the number of resident and visiting anglers increased it was soon discovered that the shores and bays from Fernandina Beach to Jacksonville had an ample quota of fish, husky redfish and seasonal migration fish in quantity, many of the species famed in more southerly areas at some time of the year. Today, fishing in this northern section is limited only by the cooler weather of the winter months, a matter of the fisherman's comfort.

St. Augustine has always had its share of anglers, as has Daytona, and today both have become attractions for the increasing number of summer anglers. Titusville, Cocoa, Rockledge, the whole Indian River country down to Fort Pierce, bring the seatrout enthusiast to their shores in search of the weighty speckled beauties that year after year topple records for poundage and quantity and keep their followers at a fever pitch of enthusiasm.

Many sailfishermen head directly for Fort Pierce, Stuart, the Palm Beaches and Miami; the bonefishermen search out the famous flats of the Keys and Gulf enthusiasts brook no argument on pompano, snook, tarpon or grouper.

It is hard to mention even this casually the outstanding fish of any one locale without some confusion because the fish are found in a variety of places along the tremendous parade of the Florida coastline, which may be measured as some 9,000 miles—counting the thousands of islands and keys—or by the more realistic figure of 1,800 miles. Florida waters add up to an incredible range of fishing possibilities.

No region of America has more fish-minded inhabitants than the residents of Florida, and the person who wants to wet a line is hardly ever out of sight of a likely spot, or out of reach of the fishing equipment with which to do so. Fishing camps are everywhere, as are boat liveries and bait houses. Docks along the "Gold Coast" are forested with the crows' nests and outriggers of enormous charterboat fleets and have their counterparts across the state at the fishing centers on the Gulf. Once again it's all anglers' choice.

A charterboat in most areas rents for from as low as $50 to as high as $75 a day; $60 could be called an average. Four is usually the maximum load of anglers permitted by the captains and this lowers costs per person to $15. Skiffs equipped with motors can be rented for from $6 to $12 a day, with those on the Gulf Coast generally slightly lower in price than on the Atlantic or in the Keys. $1 or $2 will hire a rowboat. The "party boats" charge from $4 to $6 per person for a day out on the reefs and offshore waters. Fishing piers are frequent on the Atlantic and Gulf Coasts and plentiful on the northwest Gulf Coast.

Beyond the easily approached known fishing centers are vast, lonely reaches of wilderness waters in Florida, waiting for the venturesome, more proficient angler with ample time and funds who wants to fish unfished areas with light or medium tackle. These are in the southernmost tip of Florida, where the Everglades disappear in immense, dazzling open space, with the endless low-lying Keys, unclassifiable in shape and size, dotting the wilderness with their deep green mangroves. Here in a setting of color-flaring clear waters with clouds of tropical birds moving in slow flight against the blue of empty skies, lies fishing adventure, once the rich province of the early prospector-fisherman.

To a lesser degree, these lonely stretches are duplicated by the country beginning north of Tarpon Springs, continuing beyond the Homassassa area and beyond Cedar Keys and westward around the crook of the arm of Florida's northwest Gulf Coast. Guides ply these shores, bays and rivers and the fisherman's adventures here include ascending rivers where fresh- and salt-water species vie in striking at a lure.

The West Coast of Florida can be fished intensively from piers and beaches and in bays. Countless inlets and rivers and, on calm days, the low surf of the Gulf itself, permit the use of skiffs and smaller boats so that there is extensive inshore fishing. At Fort Myers, Naples, Tampa Bay, Clearwater, Tarpon Springs, and in the seemingly endless bays of the upper Gulf Coast region, bridges, piers, and jetties are day-and-night meccas for anglers.

From the lower eastern tip of Florida's mainland stretches the Overseas Highway, going a hundred miles to sea through what has been called the nation's greatest fishbowl. Once off the mainland, a dramatic island-hopping road lies ahead of you, tracing a graceful scimitar along the outer rim of the Florida Keys, curving west through some of the state's greatest game fishing. A vast kaleidoscope of iridescent waters, palm-fringed coves, yacht basins, fishing camps and bridges arching seaward almost out of sight of land begins with the Inland Waterway cut at Jewfish Creek and ends at Key West, a hundred miles out to sea.

Fishermen, as varied a lot as a cross section of people at any main street-corner, go after their fish with every rig and gear: a scramble of spin- and fly-rod, plug and bait, cane pole and hand line—a veritable tackle store spilled along the highway. Only the newcomer is surprised at the catches hauled in daily. More than 620 varieties of fish move in the reaches of the Keys' sub-tropical waters and more than 80 of these will take a hook in some form or other.

In January a steady procession of sailing yachts, flying-deck cruisers, charterboats and sloops filters through the inland waterway to berths at private anglers' clubs and town docks at Key Largo, Tavernier, Islamorada, the Matecumbes, Marathon and Key West. These are the big-game fishermen who will fish the outer reefs for three or four months. They will follow the broad indigo path of the Gulf Stream in search of streaking wahoo and sailfish, dolphin, huge barracuda and the waterchopping schoolfish—the kings, mackerel, bonitos and tunas.

During the midwinter months the flats stretching out from the low island shorelines will fill with skiffs, waders, fly- and spin-casters, the alert guides soundlessly poling their charters across shimmering shallows for the silvery bonefish, rated by so many as a world's champion.

Florida residents never stop talking fish, but winter is not their fishing time. During this annual invasion by seasonal visitors, many local folk are too busy catering to the tourists' needs. Some of them will tell you, probably under their breath, that the spring and summer months will get you five fish for every one hung on the rack at the end of a February day. The winds of winter, often brisk, die off to a fine somnolence of calm seas in the spring; the water warms and the fish move closer shoreward.

The winter crowd, fishing from charterboat and private cruiser, hangs up many a fine record, especially in the big game division. Many are top anglers. But on the Keys an alert angler on his own, fishing by car, from bridge or ramp, or even from a skiff with an outboard, is barred only from taking a crack at the big billfish of the Gulf Stream and the larger fish of the outer reefs. Storms covering the length of the highway are rare, making it difficult for a fisherman traveling by car to be rained out. A quick run from a drifting squall into sun and calmer waters twenty miles up or down the road may well save the day.

The catch-all bait in the Keys is cut and whole mullet, but any properly used gear and lure will produce its quota of fish. By day the roster of the possible catch includes most of the Florida game fish. Darkness brings the night-feeders around bridges and shores and a new batch of fishermen moving in to places vacated by the day anglers.

The well-informed local residents know that quite a few of the best fish are primarily night-feeders, and they don't mind braving a few mosquitoes to get them. Now the snappers that teased and moved away from the most tempting bait will break up and start feeding. The great slug-jawed tarpon that lay idle and immobile all day in the shadow of bridges or clumps of mangrove overhang begin to stir and lunge across the surface of the water.

At night, on the docks, in the neon splashes of the bars that dot the dark reaches of the Keys, in the restaurants in town, the talk is of the day's fishing, the plans for tomorrow. If, instead of swapping tales, you've taken your place alongside the night-watch to jump a tarpon, you have one of fishing's greatest moments ahead of you: a huge gill-distended slab-sided fish lunging skyward, a blaze of silver in the moonlight. No motor to tire him, no guide to play your position. Just a lone, personal battle

Wonderful World of Sports Fishing

Fishing in a rowboat powered by a 3-h.p. outboard motor in most waterways of the United States would be expected to produce at best a nice string of two-pound bass or catfish. In Fabulous Florida the catch is more likely to be of a size to fill one's boat and tax one's fishing tackle faster than imagination can conjure. These fishermen said they "were doing early morning exercises before going to business" when Rube Allyn took this picture in Tampa Bay near Sunshine Skyway.

with the most versatile of all big-game fighters charging off across the water, rolling, reversing to shoot straight at bridge pilings—which you must avert at all costs. You'll watch incredible jump after jump until he tires, and then, perhaps, walk him to a ramp. There, with a silent salute, you may release him for a future fray.

At Key West they're fishing late at the end of Duval Street, the main thoroughfare, and a pile of fish will probably be on the dock behind the night club before the last note of music dies. It's all around the clock on the world's longest fishing pier in the Keys area that symbolizes so much of Florida's fabulous fishing.

Fishing is an ageless sport and in America no sport—spectator or participant—approaches it in popularity. Almost 35 million fresh-water licenses will be issued in the United States this year. At least another 10 million will also fish: old folk and children, fishermen who are not required to purchase licenses or who ignore the official regulations. These, combined with the army of salt-water anglers, add up to a roster of participants and a total expenditure that tower above the figures for any other sport in sports-minded America.

Of all the states or areas of which the very name brings to mind the spectacular game fish of the nation, Florida stands luminous and fabled. Almost seven million tourists will flow into Florida this year. Of these, it has been estimated that more than 60 per cent will go fishing at some time during their stay. Add to this the resident anglers of Florida, and it becomes a never-ending wonder that day after day and year after year, catches large and small, some even record-breaking, pour onto the docks with the close of the day, passing into a pleasant and colorful history of memory, story and picture. That the fish continue to survive is a miracle: the miracle of Florida waters.

Tackle Requirements

Since The Book of Florida Fishing is designed chiefly for the average fisherman as an easy reference aid for identification of Florida fish and for learning the most rewarding methods of catching them, the discussion of tackle and rigging which follows is not a technical one. For more exhaustive explanation of tackle and gear, weights of rods and tips, balancing of rods and lines, the angler should turn to other publications such as Fishing Digest.

There is no type of rod, from a simple cane pole to huge trolling rods equipped with keg-size Fin-Nor reels and 39-thread line, that won't take some species of Florida fish. On the other hand, there is no catchall rod suitable for Florida waters. Bonefish, for instance, are often fished with fly-rods by the expert, and also with spin-gear, with saltwater casting rods equipped with level-wind reels or service reels with drags. Star-drag reels in varying sizes are used on some forty or more Florida gamesters. Even a fresh-water bass-rod, if you want to take the always-present chance of meeting up with the unexpected "big fellow," will do well enough for seatrout and snapper and dozens of others of the smaller species.

If a charterboat is used, sound, suitable tackle is included in the day's cost. It is also probably superior to that a newcomer might obtain on his own. Rigging of baits is deftly achieved by the charterboat captains, with long years of fishing experience behind them; the uninitiated can learn more from a quarter-hour spent observing them using proven methods than from days spent poring over charts and diagrams.

For the major number of anglers who come to Florida to search out the flashing gamesters and are little interested in breaking records or excelling in tournament competition and who use skiffs or fish from bridges, piers and shores, the right tackle is largely a matter of choice. It can be easily selected according to the size and species of fish sought or, after learning "the hard way," finding out first-hand what is needed in local waters, where at any unexpected moment, while fishing for the wily mangrove snapper with the fresh-water rod you brought from home, a surging four-foot barracuda smashes in for the kill!

The soundest recommendation, and one offered as an aid to the visiting angler's pocketbook and peace of mind, is to wait to purchase tackle until you arrive in Florida and know exactly what you will fish for and where. If guides or charterboats are not to be used, a visit to any of the innumerable tackle stores or bait houses which sell or rent tackle is a sensible procedure. In Florida, possibly more than in many salt-water fishing areas, the tackle stores, docks, fishing camps and bait houses are, for the most part, operated by knowledgeable persons thoroughly familiar with the fish and fishing conditions of their own vicinity.

For the angler who prefers to equip himself with a working minimum of tackle, the following outfits are recommended:

SALT-WATER CASTING-ROD: 5½ or 6 ft., with service reel

SALT-WATER SPIN-GEAR, with heavier monofilaments and nylons

TROLLING OR BOAT-ROD: 6 oz. or 9 oz. tip, 4/0—6/0 reel with drag.

In the following Quick Reference Chart, rod classifications are not the "club," or tournament, terms used to specify rod weights and sizes, which list "heavy," "medium" and three varying "light" classifications. The following terms are designed to be generally descriptive:

HEAVY: tip weighing more than 12 oz.
MEDIUM HEAVY: tip weighing to 12 oz.
MEDIUM: tip weighing 9 oz.
LIGHT: tip weighing not more than 6 oz.
CASTING: salt-water bait-casting rod, 6 ft. length
SURF-CASTING: regulation 6 to 7 ft. tip
SPINNING: salt-water spin-gear, heavier monofilaments and nylons
FLY-RODS: salt-water fly-rods, 9 to 9½ ft.; 200 yards or more of line.

When serious angling is undertaken in Florida, one of the most sought after fish is the mighty tarpon whose thrilling maneuvers in air and water are difficult to match. The two shown above range in weight from 160 to 180 pounds

Quick-Reference Tackle and Bait Chart for Some Principal Salt-Water Game Fish

Species	*Rods*	*Hooks and Leaders*	*Baits*
AMBERJACK	Medium heavy	5/0 to 7/0 Heavy wire	Strip, weighted feathers and strip, live pinfish, mullet.
BARRACUDA	Medium trolling, casting, heavy spinning.	4/0 to 6/0 Wire	Mullet strips, spoons, feathers with strips, plugs; cut bait poor.
BASS, CHANNEL (REDFISH	Surf-casting, casting, spinning.	4/0 to 6/0 Wire—heavy nylon	Live bait, crustaceans, spoons, plugs, bucktails.
BLUEFISH	Surf-casting, casting, spinning.	4/0, 5/0 Wire	Spoons, lead squids, feathers, cut bait, small live bait.
BONEFISH	Light casting, fly-rod, spinning.	2/0, 3/0 Light wire, heavy nylon	Live shrimp, hermit crab, feathers, jigs, bucktails.
BONITO	Medium trolling.	4/0, 5/0 Wire	Strip, weighted feathers and strip.
COBIA	Heavy casting, medium heavy.	5/0 to 7/0 Wire	Strip, spoons, feathers with strips, cut bait, live bait.
DOLPHIN	Light trolling, casting, heavy spinning.	4/0 to 7/0 Light wire, heavy nylon	Mullet strips, balao, all artificials for smaller specimens.
GROUPER	Medium trolling, casting, heavy spinning.	3/0 to 8/0 Wire	Trolled strips, weighted feathers with strips, cut bait, live bait.
JACK, CREVALLE	Casting, medium trolling, heavy spinning.	2/0 to 5/0 Wire	Trolled strips, spoons, plugs, live bait.
JEWFISH	(For larger specimens) Extra heavy and tarred rope hand line.	10/0 to 12/0 Chain leader	Whole mullet, pigfish, pinfish.
KINGFISH	Medium trolling, heavy casting.	5/0 to 7/0 Long wire	Weighted feathers, strip bait, lead squid, spoons, live bait.
LADYFISH	Light casting, fly-rod, light spinning.	1/0, 2/0 Light wire, nylon	Jigs, flies, plugs, small live bait
MACKEREL, SPANISH	Light trolling, casting, spinning.	2/0 to 4/0 Long wire	Feathers, small feathers and strips, spoons, plugs, small live bait.
PERMIT	Heavy casting, medium, heaviest spinning.	4/0, 5/0 Wire, heavy nylon	Hermit crab, crawfish, live shrimp, bucktails.
POMPANO	Light casting, spinning	1/0, 2/0 Nylon	Jigs, sand fleas, smallest spoons, small streamers.

Quick-Reference Tackle and Bait Chart for Some Principal Salt-Water Game Fish

Species	*Rods*	*Hooks and Leaders*	*Baits*
SAILFISH	Medium trolling, light trolling.	8/0, 9/0 Wire	Whole threaded mullet, balao, mullet strips, bonito belly-strips.
SEATROUT, SPOTTED	Light casting, spinning, cane pole, fly-rod.	2/0 to 4/0 Nylon, light wire	Small live bait, live shrimp, plugs, streamers, numerous small artificials.
SHEEPSHEAD	Light casting, cane pole.	2/0, 3/0 Wire, heavy nylon	Fiddler crabs, hermit crabs, shrimp.
SNAPPER, MANGROVE	Light casting, spinning, fly-rod.	1/0 to 4/0 Light wire, nylon	Shrimp, cut bait, small live bait, small artificials.
SNOOK	Heavy casting, heavy spinning.	4/0, 5/0 Wire, heavy nylon	Live shrimp, jigs, live bait, spoons, bucktails, plugs.
TARPON	Medium trolling, heavy casting, heavy spinning and fly-rods for smaller specimens.	4/0 to 7/0 Wire, heavy nylon	Live mullet, pinfish, menhaden, crab, plugs, spoons, feathers.
WAHOO	Medium to heavy trolling.	5/0 to 8/0 Wire	Bonito belly-strips, whole mullet and strips, balao.

Not all denizens of the deep are caught on hook and line. This baby Whale was captured by a bather in the Gulf of Mexico off Pass-a-Grille. Actually it was not a capture. The Whale was looking for his mother, and the portly gentleman, seen through the weak eyes of the 500-pound infant, wa s the nearest thing to happiness the "little" fellow could find.

Salt-Water Sport Fishes of Florida

ALBACORE (see Tuna, Atlantic Blackfin)

ALBACORE, FALSE (*see* Tuna, Little)

AMBERJACK

BARRACUDA, GREAT

BASS
- CHANNEL (Redfish)
- STRIPED

BLUEFISH

BONEFISH

BONITO
- ATLANTIC
- OCEANIC

BROADBILL (see Swordfish)

CATFISH, GAFF-TOPSAIL

CERO (*see* Mackerel)

CHIRO (*see* Ladyfish)

COBIA

CONEY (*see* Grouper, Coney)

CREVALLE (*see* Jack, Crevalle)

CROAKER

DEVILFISH (*see* Ray, Manta)

DOLPHIN

DRUM, BLACK

FLOUNDER, SOUTHERN

FLUKE (*see* Flounder, Southern)

GROUPER
- BLACK
- CONEY
- GAG
- NASSAU
- RED
- ROCK HIND
- YELLOW
- WARSAW (*see* Jewfish, Black)

GRUNT
- BLACK MARGATE
- BLUE-STRIPED
- FRENCH
- GRAY
- MARGATE
- PIGFISH
- PORKFISH
- WHITE
- YELLOW (*see* French)

JACK
- CREVALLE
- HORSE-EYE
- YELLOW

JEWFISH
- BLACK
- SPOTTED

KINGFISH (*see* Mackerel, King)

LADYFISH

MACKEREL
- CERO
- KING
- PAINTED (*see* Mackerel, Cero)
- SPANISH

MANTA (*see* Ray, Manta)

MARLIN
- BLUE
- WHITE

MULLET

MUTTONFISH (*see* Snapper, Mutton)

PERMIT

POMPANO
- AFRICAN
- COMMON
- ROUND

PORGY
- GRASS
- JOLT-HEAD
- LITTLE-HEAD
- SOUTHERN

PORKFISH (*see* Grunt, Porkfish)

RAYS
- MANTA
- SPOTTED EAGLE
- STING

REDFISH (see Bass, Channel)

ROBALO (*see* Snook)

RUNNER
- BLUE
- RAINBOW

SAILFISH, ATLANTIC

SEATROUT
- SAND
- SILVER
- SPOTTED

SHAD

SHARKS
- GREAT BLACK-TIPPED
- HAMMERHEAD
- LESSER BLACK-TIPPED
- MAKO
- MAN-EATER
- NURSE
- THRESHER
- TIGER

SHEEPSHEAD

SNAPPER
- DOG
- LANE
- MANGROVE
- MUTTON
- RED
- SCHOOLMASTER
- YELLOWTAIL

SNOOK

SPOTTED TROUT (*see* Seatrout, Spotted)

SWORDFISH, BROADBILL

TARPON

TRIPLETAIL

TUNA
- ALLISON (*see* Tuna, Atlantic Yellowfin)
- ATLANTIC BLACKFIN
- ATLANTIC YELLOWFIN
- BLUEFIN
- LITTLE

WAHOO

WEAKFISH (*see* Seatrout)

WHITING
- SILVER
- SOUTHERN

YELLOWTAIL (*see* Snapper, Yellowtail)

One of Florida's most valuable gamefish,—and known to the fewest people, is the Sturgeon. The rivers of West Florida are populated by this fish, rather thinly, it is true—and few of them take a bait. The fish pictured above weighed 15 pounds and was caught on a worm by a St. Petersburg angler. When Rube Allyn took this photograph on the Tampa Bay waterfront it was published in The Times—and came as a surprise to many sports fishermen.

Florida Gamefish

IN THE FOLLOWING LISTING OF THE SPORT FISHES OF FLORIDA, THE FIRST NAME THAT APPEARS IS THE COMMON NAME (ACCORDING TO THE STANDARD CHECK LIST). THE LINE BELOW CARRIES THE SCIENTIFIC NAME, AND THE THIRD LINE CONTAINS THE COMMON FLORIDA NAME OR NAMES.

Amberjack

Seriola dumerili

AMBERJACK

Identification

A blackish stripe runs from the mouth across the eye to the dorsal, plainly discernible on first removing the fish from the water. A golden sheen on the sides is noticeable. The back is grayishblue to purple, the body heavily tubular in shape.

Location

Found in greatest numbers on the middle Florida Gulf Coast and on the reefs of the lower Keys. Amberjack is not a shoreline fish, preferring water 15 feet or more in depth over outer coral reefs or shale. It is not likely to school but does group around wrecks and feed-rich rock clusters. The largest amberjack are almost always solitary.

Methods of Fishing, Habits

Best methods are trolling, still fishing with live bait.

The amberjack will come up from coral formations to strike spoons, feathers and strip bait. Trolling lures are often weighted to run deep. When still fishing over reefs, live mullet, grunts and pinfish are best bait.

This is a world record Amberjack, 138½ pounds, the largest speciman ever caught on hook and line and photographed. The fisherman is Harry C. Winslow, (right) 315 Lester Road, Springfield, Pa. The professional guide assisting him in the catch is Captain Henry Clifford, Islamorada. The world record since 1955 has been 120 pounds. The catch was made off Alligator Light, fishing with cut bait on the bottom.

The strike of the amberjack is always heavy and fast, with a boring or sounding action immediately following. Because the fish is aggressive and fast in its charge for the bottom, medium-heavy tackle is necessary for all but the most skilled angler. A hard set of the hook at the moment of strike should be made when trolling. If live bait is used, the fish should be permitted a ten-foot run before setting the hook.

Caution should be observed after a long, tough fight well below the surface. After an apparent stalemate between angler and fish, an amberjack may seem to give up and allow itself to be hauled near the surface. This is often only a preface to a savage final run. At this point, other amberjack may often be seen rising with the hooked fish in what can be a "suicidal curiosity." Any handy lure then can be jigged directly in the face of the curious fish and they'll often strike.

Edibility

Poor. Should be released.

Weights

World record: 120½ lbs. Florida record: 106 lbs. Average 15-25 lbs.

Florida Gamefish

Barracuda, Great

Sphyraena barracuda

BARRACUDA, 'CUDA

Identification

The barracuda has a long, pike-shaped body, dull to bright silver sides, off-white belly, black-smudged fins. Black markings usually show in varying numbers on the sides.

The mouth is large, revealing fierce, jagged teeth, and the lower jaw protrudes, creating a tough, aggressive appearance. Its thick scales are covered with a heavy, protective slime.

Location

Barracuda are most numerous in reef waters, but they are found in the Gulf Stream, in bays and near bridges. They move into shore waters during the late-spring spawning periods. They are likely to be solitary and of great size when prowling the Stream and large-sized in small, loose schools on the reefs. In shallow water and along shorelines, they often travel in pairs.

They are frequent in Florida on the East Coast from Titusville south, in the Bay of Florida and on the lower Gulf Coast. The greatest concentrations are found in the Keys, the Dry Tortugas and the Marquesas.

Methods of Fishing, Habits

Best methods are trolling, light-tackle casting.

Because the barracuda is often taken while trolling with heavy tackle for larger fish, there has been a tendency to underestimate its magnificent abilities. It is aggressive, will strike bright spoons and plugs, often giving the impression that it is striking to kill a moving lure as much in anger or for the sake of fight as to satisfy its hunger. Metal-headed yellow or white feathers with a narrow mullet strip or pork-rind appended prove excellent lures. On the Keys, especially in late spring, barracuda can be rewardingly fished from shorelines or bridges and across flats, with light casting rods and heavier spinning outfits.

The strike is fast and slashing. In shallow water on light tackle barracuda go into a fine aerial performance after a charging run that churns the surface. Contrary to legend, they do not molest waders or swimmers, but remain wary and motionless in shallow waters near the surface. Curiosity and the expectation of an easy meal will put them into fast action, however, when they spot a hooked fish, and anglers who are wading should exercise caution in bringing a fish to gaff.

Live bait is an easy but less satisfying method where there is any concentration of barracuda. Cut bait is not recommended.

Pliers or heavy gloves should always be used when removing hooks from barracuda in order to protect the angler from any serious gashes inflicted by their snapping jaws.

The savage Barracuda, its jaw filled with jagged, memacing teeth, is ever willing to do battle. Oftener than not, as evidenced by the example shown above, the fight is a losing one for the fish. On medium tackle, especially in shallow waters, the Barracuda, is a fine aerial performer.

Because of their great numbers, their readiness to attack and their habit of pouncing on baits designed for other game fish, early Florida anglers have been wanton in their destruction of the barracuda. Today, there is a tendency to appreciate its "always-ready-for-a-fight" quality in game fishing. Many anglers now make a practice of releasing surplus fish.

Edibility

Controversial. Long considered poisonous Florida residents now eat barracuda in quantity, and it appears on the menus of many good restaurants under its own or another name. Stories of "barracuda poisoning" persist, however, and no less an authority than Dr. G. Walton Smith has stated there is a possible incidence of 1 in 20,000 which may possess harmful qualities. Flesh good. Fish should be skinned and filleted.

Weights

World record: 103¼ pounds. Average: 5-10 lbs.; in reefs and Gulf Stream, to 50 lbs. May be 5-6 feet long on the Keys and in the Dry Tortugas and the Marquesas.

Florida Gamefish

Bass, Channel

Sciaenops ocellatus

REDFISH, CHANNEL BASS

Identification

A large black spot at the base of the tail fin is an easy identifying mark of the redfish. Only rarely does more than one spot occur.

The redfish is copper or bronze-colored in Florida waters. The body is heavy and powerful, the tail, squared-off.

Fishermen used to taking redfish in more northerly Atlantic waters and designating them there as "red drum" or "red bass" will find the name "redfish" used most extensively in Florida. The correct term, "channel bass," is used only rarely.

Location

Redfish are year-round residents of Florida waters, and are more abundant along Florida coastlines than in any other area. Migrations take place northward on both coasts of Florida in the early spring months, southward in the fall. In the Ten Thousand Islands, on the ocean beaches, in the bays of the Indian River country of the Keys, along much of Florida's mid-Gulf Coast, the redfish is found sufficiently the year round to place the migratory redfish in the "dividend" class.

Methods of Fishing, Habits

Best methods are bait casting in surf, trolling near bottom, plug casting in bays, inlets or flats.

The redfish is chiefly a bottom feeder, and in the Atlantic stays just beyond the breaker line. It should be fished in this area on an incoming tide, at which time it moves shoreward in search of food. The edge of any ocean slough, shell bed or cut will be especially productive.

In Florida Bay, the Ten Thousand Islands, the back country of the Keys, along the rivers and inlets of both coasts, plug casting and the use of streamers are both remunerative. It should be remembered that the redfish is a comparatively slow striker, both on artificial baits and live bait or crustaceans. Ample time should be allowed for the fish to take hold of natural baits, especially if not in the surf, and a fractional delay should be employed in setting the hook in plug or streamer fishing.

The redfish never jumps and you can safely assume that after it has taken hold it will head for the bottom. Long runs are not usual, but steady dogged fighting, often boring bottomward is customary.

Edibility

Good to excellent. Widely used commercially. A splendid chowder fish.

Weights

World record: 83 lbs. Florida average: 5-20 lbs.

Channel Bass, or Redfish, as they are known in many localities offer the greatest sport for light tackle casting. They are strong and determined fighters. This string of matched Reds weighed about four pounds average, were taken with live shrimp near Egmont Key.

Florida Gamefish

Bass, Striped

Roccus saxatilis

STRIPED BASS, STRIPER

Identication

Pronounced dark stripes run the length of the body, the body a blending of green and silver that creates a metallic sheen. The lower jaw protrudes and the fish appears somewhat heavy-bellied.

Location

For all practical angling purposes, the northern portion of the St. Johns River and its mouth can be considered the location of striped bass in Florida, in the late fall and early winter months.

Methods of Fishing, Habits

Best methods are trolling, casting, still fishing.

This great game fish, highly prized on both the Atlantic and Pacific Coasts by surf anglers, is caught by the usual trolling methods, using spoons and feathers or still-fished, using mullet, shrimp and crab.

Because of its closely circumscribed location (in any appreciable quantity) and its appearance when the temperature of the area may be, for Florida, relatively cold, this fighting fish receives little attention from visiting anglers and is sought chiefly by resident fishermen.

Edibility

Excellent. Fine for baking.

Weights

World record: 73 lbs. Florida average: 5-15 lbs.

Bluefish are considered to be the most exciting of game for many fishermen. They are great fighters for their size and take a variety of lures. This string was lured by a redhead surface plug. They average about two pounds apiece.

Bluefish

Pomatomus saltatrix

BLUEFISH, BLUES

Identification

The back of the bluefish is a bright greenish-blue that shades to silvery sides and an almost white belly. The fish is sleek and streamlined, scales are small, teeth are numerous and extremely sharp.

Location

Bluefish school in great numbers off the Florida Atlantic Coast in March and early April, on their northward migration, and again in September on their return. In recent years their number has been increasing on the Gulf Coast. Florida fishermen take most of their blues in the surf, inlets and bay channels.

Methods of Fishing, Habits

Best methods are light-tackle casting, surf-casting, trolling, spin-casting.

No fish has a sharper strike for its weight than the blue. The slashing rush is so fast that instantaneous hooking is a necessity. The hit-and-run characteristic of blues makes the use of live bait during bluefish runs a time-wasting method.

Schools advertise their appearance by their incredibly voracious and vicious slaughter of schools of mullet, pilchard and menhaden. This sends the hapless smaller fish into a panic that churns the water and brings clouds of gulls from miles around. When feeding, they are the most greedy of all fish. They will strike any shiny object in their race to kill and feed, thus making themselves the easy victims of freshly scraped lead squids, spoons and small metal-headed feather lures.

The sharp teeth and snapping jaws of the bluefish require the use of a leader, preferably three feet or more in length. Care should be exercised in unhooking the fish.

In making a cast in surf or in a channel, no retrieve of the lure can be too fast. Tackle should be light and easily maneuverable.

If fishing in an inlet or in channel waters, a good trick is to have a bucket of fish scaps handy. When the blues move in chum tossed in the water will hold them in the immediate area. Fast-worked lures will produce strikes as rapidly as the lure can be returned to the water.

When schools are not visible or revealed by clouds of birds above, trolling with spoons or lead squids to locate fish is recommended.

Edibility

Excellent. A rich, somewhat dark flesh. However, the fish should be iced within an hour or so of catching, as spoilage sets in rapidly in subtropical climates.

Weights

World record: 21 lbs., 3 oz. Florida average: 2-2½ lbs.

Bonefish

Albula vulpes
BONEFISH

Identification

Although coloration of the bonefish is variable, it always shows heavy, rich bright silver scales of a dazzling beauty. During certain phases of changing color, horizontal stripes are pronounced, these markings at least faintly visible even at the height of its flashing-silver phases.

The mouth is comparatively small, the tail widely forked, the nose rounded and extended over the mouth. The greenish back of the bonefish is broad, the body heavily tubular, giving it a well deserved appearance of tremendous strength.

Location

The bonefish is strictly a shallow-water fish and its area of habitation, for all practical angling purposes, can be considered the flats, bars and sandy stretches of the southern tip of the mainland and the length of the Keys.

Methods of Fishing, Habits

Many expert bonefishermen employ highly individualized methods in seeking this game fish. The best recommendation to the angler seeking bonefish for the first time is to hire one of the many excellent guides specializing in bonefishing in the Key Largo, Islamorada or Marathon areas and spend a day on the flats fishing and observing their methods. (The rates there are about half those of charterboats).

As bonefish move in over flats with incoming tides, the fishing time is considered to be from when the tide is halfway up until the beginning of the ebb. They are chiefly crustacean feeders and shrimp and finny crabs are top baits.

In the often crystalline waters of the Keys, the bonefish can be observed at a considerable distance "tailing" and "mudding" — feeding head down with their tails protruding in a slow-waving motion and stirring up tiny clouds of sand or mud. Guides pole shallow-draft skiffs, slowly searching out the fish, introducing an exciting hunting element.

An early method of bonefishing was chumming — creating a small slick of crushed crustaceans on a tide moving in over the flats. Early bonefishermen filled small canvas sacks with fiddler, blue and hermit crabs, mashing them against the boat side, then waited for the fish to move up the slick before making their casts. Today, sighting the fish and making direct casts is the usual procedure.

Inasmuch as bonefish are constantly on the move while feeding, the angler can reverse the field of pursuing the fish and await their appearance in a selected spot, placing himself either on or near the shore of a known feeding flat and making blind casts, or wading quietly over a flat and fishing, trout-stream fashion.

Most often mistaken in identification are BONEFISH. Two species, *Albula Vulpes* and *Flops saurus* have the common name of "Bonefish." On the left above, is a true bonefish, prized gamefish of shallow waters in the Florida Keys. On the right a false bonefish, commonly called LADYFISH. The Ladyfish is a gamefish of the first degree. Experts have written that the "Lady" is America's greatest gamefish, pound for pound. No other fish can leap as high when hooked.

Quiet movements are absolutely necessary, and casts should be placed well ahead of the oncoming fish, as they are extremely scary, "spook" easily and, once alarmed, disappear from view with amazing speed.

Fly-fishing and spinning-tackle enthusiasts have brought in the use of flies and tiny streamers—white and yellow bucktails are favorites—and, of course, with this expert approach, direct casts to sighted fish are a necessity. Reels that will take 250 yards of filament line are a prerequisite in handling the long searing run of the bonefish when first hooked.

The strike of the bonefish when shrimp or crab is used is most deceptive. There is often a slight lifting of the bait. Once the fish feels the barb or senses a hook an incredible, explosive charge for freedom ensues. The initial run is often as much as 250 feet, even 400 feet, before the fish slows or turns.

Bonefish are also night feeders. They can be successfully fished, especially on moonlight nights, by blind casting with shrimp on a known feeding flat.

Edibility

Only fair, with an excessive quantity of bones. They should be released unless desired for mounting or for an entry as a citation fish.

World record: 18 lbs. 2 ozs. Florida record: 15 lbs. Average: Keys, 5-7 lbs.

Bonito, Atlantic

Sarda sarda

COMMON BONITO, BONITO

Identification

Sharply defined black wavy lines flow upward from the bright silvery sides of the fish across the deep-hued blue back. The shape of the fish is tubular, streamlined, following the general body outlines of the oceanic bonito and little tuna. Several large spike-like teeth show in the lower jaw. Completely scaled. Does not have the beauty and brilliance of the oceanic bonito.

Location

The bonito is a deep-water fish, rarely found inside the outer reefs or the Gulf Stream. Somewhat more frequently found on the Atlantic Coast of Florida than in Gulf waters.

Methods of Fishing, Habits

Best methods are deep trolling, surface trolling.

The bonito travels in large schools well below the surface except when feeding. Favorite foods are sardines, menhaden and other small fishes.

The strike of this not overlarge fish has been compared to hooking a heavy stationary object. Their speed of swimming ranks them with the fleetest fish. Their first run after the startling impact of their strike is long and determined. Many anglers, although usually hitting them with oversize tackle, believe they are playing a fish two or three times the size of what they see when the fish is surfaced.

When it has been ascertained that a hooked bonito is one of a school and not a stray, light tackle can go into play. Undersurface lures — feathers, plugs, spoons — will provide fast, tough action.

Bonito belly-strips rank at the top of desired baits for larger Gulf Stream fish.

Edibility

Dark meat, heavy with blood. Not appetizing unless brined, then boiled. Fair flavor when canned.

Weights

Florida average: 3 - 5 lbs.

Bonito, Oceanic

Katsuwonus pelamis

ARCTIC BONITO (a Florida Misnomer) and BONITO

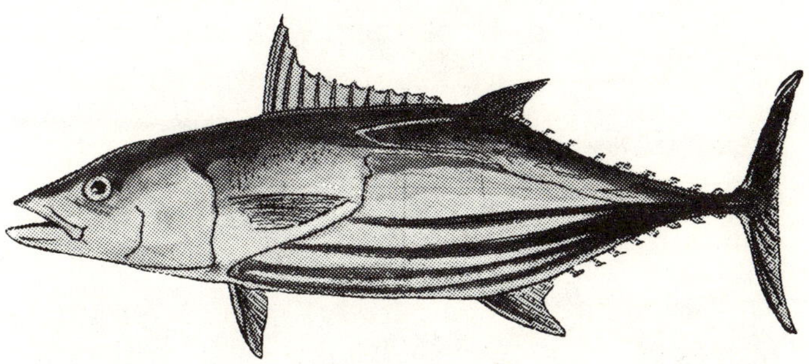

Identification

This member of the little tuna family is the most colorful of the lot. Dark horizontal stripes start at the pectoral fin and flow with a slightly upward sweep at the tail, making a sharp contrast against the pinkish-yellow belly and sides. The back is ocean blue with irregular serrated markings from the second dorsal to the tail. Somewhat thicker, less streamlined through the body than the Atlantic bonito.

Location

The very location of the oceanic bonito belies the long-used name in Florida of Arctic bonito. This little tuna is definitely a warm-water fish, its greatest frequency from the mid-Atlantic Coast south. Further, not too many are taken until the waters warm in the early spring. They travel with other bonitos and at times move in closer shoreward or on reefs.

Methods of Fishing, Habits

Best method is surface trolling.

For the most part, the oceanic bonito follows the pattern of the Atlantic bonito, possibly not quite as fast or as enduring in its fight, although on light tackle it will be hard to distinguish any difference. Takes the same lures and baits as those used for Atlantic bonito.

Edibility

Considered somewhat more tasty than the Atlantic bonito, but certainly no delicacy.

Weights

World record: 39 lbs., 15 oz. Florida average: 3 - 5 lbs. Reported to 25 lbs.

Catfish, Gaff-Topsail

Bagre marinus

GAFF-TOPSAIL CAT

Identification

The gaff-topsail is most easily distinguished from the sea cat by an elongated dorsal fin with a slender filament thrusting upward from the front spine and trailing pectoral fin. The tail is a deep, curved fork. The back is blue-grayish, shading off to a light belly.

Location

Most frequent in inlets, bays, channels. However, they also feed along beaches. Found in all Florida waters.

Methods of Fishing, Habits

Best method is casting, with small artificials, shrimp, cut bait.

For many years fishermen relegated the gaff-topsail to the annoyance-and-trash division, especially bottom-fishermen who sought food fish. But the hard strike of the fish and the fact that, unlike the despised sea cat or common cat, it will take a fast grab at plugs and other artificial baits, have gradually elevated this species in the eyes of sports fishermen. Casting in low surf waters on light tackle offers the best play this fish provides. They are caught at all seasons.

Edibility

Now known to be an acceptable table-fish. They are not scavengers like their close relatives the sea cats.

Weights

Up to 7 lbs. Florida average: 2½-4 lbs.

Cobia

Rachycentron canadus

COBIA

Identification

The back shows a deep cocoa or charcoal brown color, shading to an off-white belly. Anglers familiar with cobia in the central Atlantic area will note an over-all lighter shade

Cobia, the most sought-after foodfish, by sportsmen who have tried them all, range up to 75 pounds. This 60-pounder gave the boys quite a battle on a light casting rod. The catch was made by floating a live shiner close to a range light beacon.

in cobia caught in Florida waters. The fish is shaped somewhat similarly to a snook, with a short, flattened head and a protruding lower jaw. The mouth is large. A stripe runs straight from the snout through the eye to the tail, with no waver in the line, however, such as the snook marking.

Location

All Florida waters. Appearance of cobia in quantity has always been uncertain but seems seasonal to some degree. They show with fair frequency from Canaveral down through Stuart in spring and summer, but the Gulf Coast is generally far more productive than the Atlantic. They are taken the year-round from the Ten Thousand Islands to Tarpon Springs, are considered incidental in the Keys.

It is in northwest Florida, however, from Carabelle, across Apalachicola Bay, at Panama City and Pensacola, where a sensational run of huge cobia, ranging in weight from 25 to 75 lbs., evidences a strong migratory movement beginning in early April and continuing into early summer. Cobia are usually considered an offshore fish. In the Gulf areas, however, they are found in channels and at river mouths, with areas such as Lower Tampa Bay considered choice grounds. In the northwest Gulf country, fishing piers report tremendous catches during spring runs.

Methods of Fishing, Habits

Best methods are floated live baits, trolling. In northwest Gulf area over known grounds, cut and live bait fished on bottom.

The strike of the cobia at trolled strips, plugs, weighted feathers is jolting. On live baits, shrimp and crab, the attack is a running smash, followed by charging runs with sharp yankings that form a constant threat to tackle. Cobia seem to sense danger when brought within sight of a boat or bridge pier and go into a frenzy of head-down fighting even after they seem to have reached exhaustion. Sudden slack lines should be most carefully watched and not necessarily considered as a loss of the fish, as cobia change their direction without warning and streak toward the boat as rapidly as for the open sea. Their entire fight is rough-and-tumble, demanding the strictest attention from the angler. They are not a light-tackle fish except for the most expert fishermen.

When trolling, speed of troll should be very rapid. When a fish is boated, the area should be immediately circled for companions. When fishing with floats or on the bottom the angler must strike instantaneously with the lunge of the fish.

Plug-casting and spin-gear are used by the experienced during cobia runs, around buoys where cobia often group and in other waters they are known to frequent. These gears should always be of the heavier weights.

Edibility

Excellent. White, fine-grained flesh.

Weights

World record: 102 lbs. Florida average: 15 lbs. 40-75 lbs. not unusual during spring runs in the northwest area.

Croaker

Micropogon undulatus

CROAKER

Identification

Dull irregular vertical markings show beneath a light copperish sheen. Dull brown spots dot the length of the upper body. Upper jaw is slightly overhung.

On being brought to the surface and removed from the water a protesting croaking from the fish is most audible.

Location

All Florida waters.

Croakers are usually taken from surf and swash channels. They are also found in inlets and bays but always over sandy or shell bottoms.

Methods of Fishing, Habits

Best methods are still fishing, bait-casting in surf.

Fishermen used to the incredible quantities of croakers in other areas, such as the York River or Chesapeake Bay country, will not find them nearly so numerous or so large in Florida. Here they are an incidental fish caught along the Gulf or Atlantic beaches or in bays and river mouths over shell or sand bottoms, generally while fishing for other species.

It was long thought croakers would strike only on natural baits on the bottom. However, it has been discovered that small lures on spinning- or plug-casting rods, allowed to rest on the bottom and then put into sudden motion, will bring strikes.

Inasmuch as the croaker usually runs in the smaller sizes in Florida, they can be considered only a fair fighter on very light tackle. Their strike is fairly tough, but their endurance is mediocre.

Edibility

Good, flesh firm and succulent.

Weights

Florida average: 1 lb. Reported to 5 lbs.

Florida Gamefish

Dolphin

Coryphaena hippurus
DOLPHIN

Identification

A magnificently hued fish which draws ecstatic tributes for its exceptional grace, its sleek lines and riotous splash of flaring colors.

The long dorsal, extending from the head the length of the body, is a vivid, electric blue. Bright purple dots mark the entire body, sea-green on the upper back, shading to yellows and silver below, with red tinges on the fins and gill-covers.

Attempting to pin down accurate coloration markings of the dolphin is an impossible task inasmuch as variations are incredibly frequent, subject to the slightest emotional change. While ranging free, the dolphin in Florida waters could be said to show an over-all silver, blue and green coloration. Immediately on being hooked, flashes of yellow, deep blue, green and gold flush the entire body. It has been noted that from the time a dolphin is free-swimming, through the experience of a strike, hooking, boating and especially as it dies, fifteen to twenty washes of brilliant color flash in quick succession over its body.

Male and female dolphin are most easily distinguishable. The male or bull dolphin has a squared-off head, the forehead rising straight from the mouth. The head of the female is more rounded, conventionally formed.

Location

Dolphin range in and at the edge of the Gulf Stream and in immediately adjacent offshore waters. They are located most frequently on the Florida East Coast from early spring to August. They appear in lesser numbers in the Gulf well offshore. Although far more numerous in the spring and early summer months, they are taken the year-round in Florida.

Methods of Fishing, Habits

Best methods are trolling, light-tackle casting after locating a school.

Salt-water anglers never fail to thrill to the shout of the captain, "Here come the dolphin!" The keen-eyed dolphin start tearing after trolled baits, whole mullet, strips, feathers, spoons—from as much as 60 feet—flashing silver arcs in the air, moving with lightning speed to pounce on baits and romp off at unexpected angles in searing runs and spectacular aerial leaps. It is not at all unusual, if three lines are being trolled, to have a single dolphin plunge off with all three with what seems to the often bewildered fishermen like instantaneous action, so fast is the racing strike at the baits.

Further confusion for the inexperienced dolphin fisherman is afforded by slack lines following an obvious strike. Dolphin will often take a run straight for the boat or angle off to a parallel charge. They take to the air at unexpected moments, and even when their rapidly changing hues are making rainbow whorls at boatside, high aerial flips can be expected.

Dolphin are among the most curious of all fish. A floating box, a patch of weed, in fact, any object in the water which offers shade and attracts small fish, will attract dolphin from great distances. In early years off Key West, fishermen tossed laced-together packing boxes overboard and returned to them a couple of hours later with the fair certainty that dolphin would be clustered beneath.

This curiosity can be made suicidal for dolphin. When dolphin are found beneath a weed patch, light-casting tackle should go into action. When one angler of a party hooks a dolphin, he should allow it to remain in the water after subduing it until his fishing companions get a chance at one of the half-dozen or more dolphin that will cluster around the hooked fish. If the removal of the hooked fish is delayed, successful fishing can often be continued for an hour or more.

In schools, where the average size of the dolphin is from four to six pounds, larger ones can many times be located by fishing at greater depths. Away from schools of smaller dolphin, larger specimens, in the 20 to 35 lb.-class, travel in pairs.

Edibility

A preferred delicacy by many. Easily stripped for broiling or frying.

Weights

World record: 75½ lbs. School average: 4 - 6 lbs. To 50 lbs. in Florida.

Drum, Black

Pogonias cromis
DRUM

Identification

A dark metallic brassy sheen shows over this chunky, heavy-bodied fish. The fins are black, and wide dark vertical markings band the body from dorsal to the off-white belly. Numerous barbels, or tiny beards, extend from the lower jaw.

Location

The drum is a shoreline fish, inhabiting inlets, river mouths and beaches. It is most frequent along the Atlantic Coast from Cocoa north and especially numerous along the beaches of the St. Augustine area. Roughly, the same latitude can be considered a good drum area on the Gulf Coast.

Methods of Fishing, Habits

Best method is still fishing on bottom with crustaceans. The drum feeds chiefly over hard shell-bottom — oysters, clams, mussels, crab, shrimp — all favorate foods. They will take small fish, but not as readily.

Their liking for river mouths, docks and pilings pinpoints their location for drum fishermen, although surf fishing in the locations mentioned above can be very productive, especially from early spring to midsummer. They should always be bottom-fished.

The strike of the drum is slow and casual, but once hooked, it fights strongly. In bays and rivers, the action is one of determined boring down, while in the surf the drum tries seaward runs to reach the safety of deeper waters. Drum are hand-lined commercially, and sports fishermen sometimes turn to this method to seek the larger specimens where schools are known to be working around abutments, docks or bridges, thus minimizing their losses from broken lines tangled on obstructions.

Edibility

Widely used commercially, but not by the knowing sports fisherman. Meat is rather tasteless. Worms and parasites often present, harmless, but certainly not appetizing.

Weights

World record on rod and reel: 92 lbs. Average: 6 - 10 lbs. Reported to 146 lbs on hand line in Florida.

Flounder, Southern

Paralichthys lethostigmus

FLOUNDER, FLUKE

Identification

A handsome member of the fluke family, lighter in color than its northern relatives. Mot-

A catch of Black Drum which provided an exciting morning's fishing experience for these three men. They used Shedded Crabs for bait and fished over a deep oyster bar. Average single fish weight was 25 pounds for the string.

tled tail and sides with three or four large sharply defined dark spots. Usually a light greenish cast, varying considerably in depth of tone according to the bottom over which it is caught.

Location

A shoreline, bay and backwater fish, found in greatest numbers in Florida along the Gulf Coast, inside or in swash channels. It is almost always found inhabiting a sandy bottom. Taken in surf on Atlantic Coast. Rare on the Keys.

Methods of Fishing, Habits

Although often caught in daylight hours, the flounder moves close in to shore on the Gulf beaches with the fall of night and feeds heavily after dark. This propensity to seek food in the wash of shore waters has made the fish most vulnerable to waders with gigs and spears, who jacklight them in quantity along the whole Gulf Coast.

Shiners, small crabs and shrimp are excellent bait for the hook-and-line fisherman. Fluke are always fished on the bottom and bait, not artificial lures, should be used. Sport is ordinarily secondary to the pleasure of wading and searching out the fish for its splendid table value.

Edibility

Excellent.

Weights

Florida average: 2 - 2½ lbs.

Grouper, Black

Mycteroperca bonaci

BLACK GROUPER

Identification

Over-all grayish color, to brown in certain color phases, all fins, except the front dorsal, edged in black, these fin markings a sure identifying feature. Dark oblong markings form both lateral lines and vertical bars.

Location

Most common on the Gulf Coast, and on the Keys. A few caught on lower East Coast. The black grouper is an offshore fish, taken in Gulf waters over rocks located well out in the Gulf, on the Keys over outer reefs.

Methods of Fishing, Habits

Best methods are still fishing with cut or live bait in Gulf, trolling with weighted feathers and appended strips in the waters of the Keys.

A favorite of the deep-sea fishing boats in the Gulf of Mexico, Black Grouper can furnish an exciting day for the man fishing over the rail of an open party boat. This pair was part of a catch landed at Johns Pass, from the Clymer Brothers fishing fleet of "Atlanta boats." They weighed in at 40 pounds.

The strike and fight of the black grouper are the toughest of any of the grouper family. They lunge for their food, go into an immediate boring, headdown charge for jumbles of rocks and holes. The result of their charges, if not checked, means cut lines or a losing entanglement on the rocks. Thus fairly heavy tackle and an all-out effort against the fish's ocean-floor flight should be employed.

Edibility
Good, comparable to other groupers.

Weights
Florida average: 5 - 10 lbs., a 20 - 25 lb. fish is not uncommon. Reported to 50 lbs.

Grouper, Coney

Cephalopholis fulvus
CONEY GROUPER

Identification
The coney is the smallest of the grouper family, and easily identified by its usual overall bright rosy red color, thickly sprinkled with yellow dots the entire length of the body.

Location
Seldom found outside lower Keys area. Usually taken over outer reefs.

Methods of Fishing, Habits
Caught incidentally while bottom fishing.

Coneys caught on Keys reefs are small, going to a pound or so, are taken in the company of the usual bottom fish of the reefs while still fishing. Considered somewhat of a prize for beauty and scarcity.

Edibility
Fair.

Weights
Average: ¾ - 1 lb. Goes to 3 lbs.

Grouper, Gag

Mycteroperca microlepis
GAG, GAG GROUPER

Identification
The gag is slightly more streamlined and more slender than most groupers. Its coloration is pale, its light mottling looks washed-out. Usually a whitish gray to a pale greenish brown. The tail fin tip is banded in black.

Location
All Florida waters, with greatest frequency in the lower Keys area.

Methods of Fishing, Habits
Best methods are still fishing with cut or live bait, trolling with weighted feathers.

The gag has a hard, plunging strike, more endurance than many of its grouper relatives. It runs more and has less tendency to make an immediate dive for entangling rocks.

Edibility
Fair to good.

Weights
Florida average: 4-6 lbs. Reported to 25 lbs.

Grouper, Nassau

Epinephelus striatus
NASSAU GROUPER

Identification

A brightly mottled grouper, with characteristic square tail and broad vertical spotted dark bands. Mottling continues through tail.

Location

All Florida waters, becoming scarcer in the Gulf north of Tarpon Springs.

The Nassau grouper, like all members of the grouper family, is a bottom fish, found in holes near channels, over reefs and rocky bottoms.

Methods of Fishing, Habits

Nassau grouper should be fished by the same methods noted under red grouper. Chumming is most rewarding.

Edibility

Excellent. It is indistinguishable from the red grouper and the same methods of preparation and cooking should be followed.

Weights

Average: below 10 lbs. 50-pounders have been reported.

Grouper, Red

Epinephelus morio
RED GROUPER

Identification

The red grouper is reddish brown, mottled over the entire body, including the fins. The mouth is large and reveals a brilliant orange color when open. The tail is square and sturdy, characteristic of the entire grouper family.

Location

This is the most numerous grouper and is found in quantity in all Florida waters, with the Gulf Coast area providing the greatest concentrations. Market fishermen make tremendous catches from Naples to Pensacola.

The red grouper is a bottom fish, inhabiting holes and gathering in great numbers over rocky bottoms and reefs. On the Keys smaller red grouper are taken over coral in fairly shallow water. The larger grouper are found here in deeper water and this is also true of the Pensacola area, where enormous hauls are made by red-snapper fishermen. In the middle Gulf areas, locating rock or shell bottom just offshore beyond the swash channel will be productive for sports fishermen.

Methods of Fishing, Habits

Best method is bottom fishing with cut bait.

If the locations of rock, coral formations, or shell bottoms are not familiar to the fisherman seeking red grouper, the boat should be allowed to drift until such a bottom is located. The red grouper is almost always found in the company of grunts and other bottom fish, and hooking into rock or shell or catching grunts is an indication the angler has reached a grouper hole or bed. They never inhabit sandy bottoms.

For larger grouper, strip baits and feathers slowly trolled over known reefs and rocky areas will produce good catches. The larger red grouper strike with a solid thud, usually hooking themselves on the strike. The greatest danger of loss to the fisherman comes from underestimating the grouper's strength and weight immediately after the strike. Slow, even working to prevent the grouper from exercising his habit of boring down to rock, hole and cave, where he will saw off or hang up the line, should be the angler's first consideration.

The fight of the grouper is not long, once he is checked or pried up from the bottom.

Edibility

Visitors to Florida especially to the West Coast, have probably eaten more red grouper under a wider variety of names than they have any other fish. The meat is firm and tasty. Grouper should always be skinned, as the skin is tough and strong-flavored. Widely used for chowder when not steaked.

Weights

Average: 2 - 5 lbs. Reported to 40 lbs.

Grouper, Rock Hind

Epinephelus adscenionis
ROCK HIND GROUPER

Identification

The rock hind, a small member of the grouper family, in most color phases shows a measles-like profusion of red dots over the entire body, fins and a portion of the tail. The body is often a patchy dark green. Refer to yellow grouper, with which it is often confused, for differentiating characteristics.

Location

Chiefly a Keys fish, usually inhabiting outer reefs and rock piles. It is rarely taken in shallow water.

Methods of Fishing, Habits

Best methods are still fishing, deep troll. Rock hind are fish caught incidentally while bottom-fishing the Keys reefs. They do not respond to surface lures but will take feather and strip baits trolled deep.

Edibility

Fair to good.

Weights

2 - 3 lbs. Reported to 12 lbs. in Florida.

Grouper, Yellow

Mycteroperca venenosa
YELLOW GROUPER

Identification

An especially handsome member of the grouper family, heavily dotted over entire body and fins. Dots are red on the head and white belly, greenish - black over gray - green upper sides and back.

It is difficult, at times, to distinguish the yellow grouper from the rock hind. Best identifying differences are the fairly consistent color of the sides and belly of the yellow grouper, as contrasted with the patchy coloration beneath the rock hind's spots, and the shape of the tail; the yellow grouper's tail is square to slightly concave, the rock hind's more rounded.

Location

South Florida, chiefly Keys areas. The yellow grouper lives only over reefs, rock piles and around bridge abutments where bottom is heavy with shell and rock.

Methods of Fishing, Habits

Best methods are still fishing with cut or live bait. Yellow grouper follow the characteristics of their more numerous relatives in feeding and striking, are incidental in catches of bottom fishermen along the Keys.

Edibility

Fair to good.

Weights

Average: 2 - 4 lbs. Reported to 7 lbs.

Grunts

The grunts comprise a fairly large family of brilliantly-colored fish found in all Florida waters. Bottom feeders, they are usually avid and indiscriminate in their feeding, readily taking cut baits, small live baits and crustaceans.

They are sought by Florida sports-fishermen as an excellent small panfish, and are often fished on very light tackle on those windy days that confine anglers to inshore and protected waters. Several, especially the blue-striped grunt and the pigfish, are widely favored as live bait for tarpon, amberjack and other large fish, and are far more easily kept alive in bait wells for this purpose than live mullet, as mullet frantically bruise and mutilate themselves quickly in confinement.

They school over reefs and rocky bottoms, are often in the company of snapper and grouper, and are mostly sensitive to chilling temperatures, moving into deeper waters during cold snaps.

Methods of taking grunts are consistent and apply generally to all members of the grunt family — still fishing on the bottom with the baits noted above. Thus, only identifying characteristics, varying locations, edibility and weights are detailed below.

The various grunts have been dubbed a wide variety of local names by Florida fishermen. The names used here follow the Standard Check List and the most widely used common names throughout Florida.

Black Margate

Anisotremus surinamemsis

BLACK MARGATE GRUNT, POMPON

Identification

The largest of the grunt family. It is a light-gray, the fins shading from a very dark gray to black. Wide black patches on the sides give the appearance of a broad encircling band. The mouth is comparatively small and thick-lipped. The inside of the mouth is grayish-white.

The black margate is sometimes confused with black drum. Quickest identifying difference: absence of barbels beneath lower jaw.

Location

Reefs, rocky inshore bottoms, greatest frequency in lower East Coast and Keys areas.

Edibility

A splendid food fish.

Weights

Although reported to 15 - 20 lbs., the Florida angler will seldom take a black margate over 2 lbs.; average: 1 - 1¼ lbs.

Blue-Striped Grunt

Haemulon sciurus

BLUE GRUNT

Identification

Easily identified by blue stripes, sharply contrasting with yellow, running longitudinally the length of the body. Dorsal and tail fins are dark-gray to black, other fins are yellowish. The inside of the mouth is a flaring bright red, characteristic of many of the grunts.

Location

All Florida waters. It ranges more numerously in deeper waters, schooling over shell and ledges in 12 to 15 feet of water, is found in pods in deep holes near mangrove growth. A night-as well as day-feeder.

Edibility

A fine pan fish. As noted above, it is a wide-favored bait, used alive for tarpon and amberjack, Warsaw grouper and other large fish.

Weights

Florida average: ½ - ¾ lb. Known to go to 2½ lbs.

French Grunt

Haemulon flavolineatum

YELLOW GRUNT, FRENCH GRUNT

Identification

A brightly-colored grunt, with brilliant yellow stripes running the length of the gray-blue body. Fins are a golden yellow, the dorsal sometimes tinged with light blue. The mouth is the same vivid red of the blue-striped grunt.

Location

Southern East Coast and Florida Keys. Found usually over reefs and coral in company of snapper, other grunts and grouper.

Edibility

Good.

Weights

Florida average: ½ - ¾ lb., 1 lb. large.

Gray Grunt

Haemulon macrostomum

GRAY GRUNT

Identification

The gray grunt shows an over-all tarnished silver-gray color with dark stripes on upper sides. Fins are a muddy yellow. One of the smaller grunts.

Location

Not frequent anywhere but found in some quanitity in the lower Keys area. Only occasional on lower East Coast.

Edibility

Good, but usually passed up in favor of larger members of grunt family.

Weights

Florida average: ¼ - ½ lb. To 1 lb.

Margate Grunt

Haemulon album

MARGATE GRUNT

Identification

Gray-green in color, with several narrow black stripes running longitudinally on upper sides. The inside of the mouth is typically grunt-red, the fins are dark gray.

Location

Fairly frequent in the Keys area, scarce on lower mainland. Thought to move shoreward from reefs for night feeding. Margate can generally be considered to inhabit somewhat deeper waters than other members of its family.

Edibility

Good.

Weights

Margate, like the black margate, are said to go to considerable poundage, reported in the Bahamas to 8 lbs. Florida average, however, is 1 lb., occasionally taken in weights of 2 and 3 lbs.

Pigfish

Orthopristis chryopterus

PIGFISH, SAILOR'S CHOICE

Identification

The pigfish has a light, silver-blue back, shading to a silvery yellow on the sides. Blue stripes rise upward on the head, brown dots form lateral-appearing lines on lower sides. Fins are brown-dotted, outlined with black. Tail fin yellow. Inside of mouth is pale. One of the smaller grunts.

Location

All Florida waters, especially numerous on the Gulf Coast. Moves in over sand, flats and grass.

Edibility

Because it is usually taken in such small sizes, its excellent table qualities are often passed over. Like the blue-striped grunt, the pigfish is a splendid bait for larger game fish.

Weights

Florida average: ¼ - ½ lb. Reported to 1½ lbs.

White Grunt

Maeoulon plumieri

COMMON GRUNT

Identification

Back is blue to blue-gray. The head shows irregular wavy blue stripes. The body shades from grayish-blue to an off-white belly. Mouth is darkish, large, with the inside a bright red.

Location

All Florida waters. Common Gulf Coast, in the Keys, and numerous on the lower East Coast. They are frequent in bays and along sand beach areas, also show up on inner reefs and shell bottoms.

Edibility

One of the most widely-used small pan fish.

Weights

One pound average not unusual in some areas. Goes to 3 lbs.

Yellow Grunt

(*see French Grunt*)

Porkfish

Anisotremus virginicus

PORKFISH

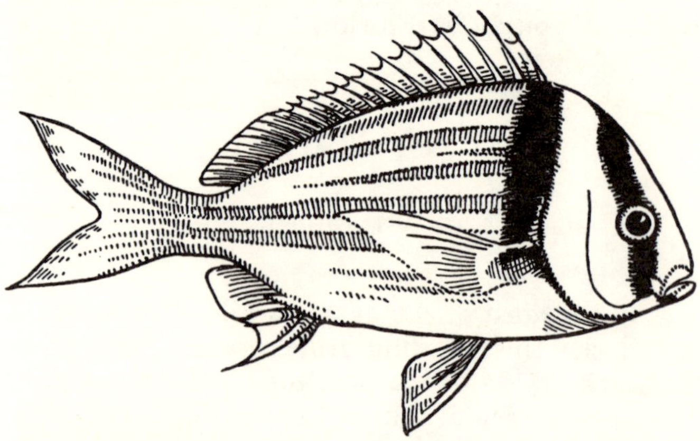

Identification

A handsome, brilliantly-marked grunt. One jet-black broad stripe runs from the front of the first dorsal down to the pectoral fin, another bands the mouth's corner with the eye and forehead. Body is yellow, heavily striped in pale blue. Belly is light silver or white. Fins are golden yellow.

Location

Found in greatest concentrations in the Keys area, occasional on lower mainland shores and East Coast. Porkfish cluster under protecting ledges on reefs, seek shell bottom, bridge and dock pilings.

Edibility

Excellent.

Weights

Average: ½ lb. Occasionally to 1, 1¼ lbs.

Florida Gamefish

There are always fish that are bigger than the "reported" size, for no one really knows how large a fish can get. This Hogfish, weighing 22 pounds was a whopping catch for the lady who is displaying it. She used a large shrimp and was fishing on the bottom,

Hogfish

Lachnolaimus maximus

HOGFISH

Identification

One of the most colorful and beautiful of the Florida reef fish, with an unusual variation of colorations. Usually the fish shows a light mahogany red, mottled with yellow irregular markings. Always present—and a sound identifying mark—is a large black spot at the back of the second dorsal. Blue patches show on the large jowls. Tendrils form the front dorsal, the upper strands streaming well back over the second dorsal. The tail is broad and squarish. The snout is piglike, which gives this handsome fish its name.

Location

For all practical angling purposes the Florida Keys can be considered the home of the hogfish. Strays are found north to Fernandina Beach.

The hogfish feeds on rock and shell bottom, over inner and outer reefs. It is never found over sand, prefers heavy sea growths that bloom near rock piles.

Methods of Fishing, Habits

Best methods are bottom fishing with shrimp, lobster.

The hogfish cannot be said to school, although several are liable to be taken over rock clusters.

Hogfish are taken by Keys fishermen while bottom fishing for the usual reef fish. Their fighting strength is far superior to many of their neighbors', and anglers will think they have hooked a larger bottom fish than appears when the fish has been surfaced. A boring action often results in line entanglement in undersea growths or on rock and if the angler is having success in landing the greatly desired hogfish, heavier lines should be used.

Edibility

A great Keys delicacy. The flesh of the hogfish is white, fine-grained, most flavorful.

Weights

Average: 3 - 5 lbs., reported to 12.

Florida Gamefish

Jack, Crevalle

Caranx hippos
JACKS, CREVALLE

Identification

The body is heavy for its length and is often confused with the many similarly colored and shaped members of the jack and pompano family. The belly is yellow. Possibly the quickest method of distinguishing it from its look-alike relatives is by its two large black spots—one on the gill cover and one on the pectoral fin. Tough bony scutes form a line to a wide-forked tail. An over-all silver and yellow sheen shows on the sides, shading off from a light-green back.

Location

Largest crevalle jack are found in the southerly areas of Florida. Their range, however, is all Florida waters. The smaller jack school in shallow water, in bays and over flats, the larger jack travel in packs up to ten or a dozen and move constantly in search of smaller fish in cuts and channels, over reefs, and along the pilings of bridges. In the Indian River and in similar river or bay areas, a school or pack of jack can often be sighted, cutting and slashing mullet for as far as the eye can see. So persistent is their pursuit and killing that mullet have been known to toss themselves on a shore or attempt to ascend pilings in their terror.

Methods of Fishing, Habits

Best methods are trolling, plug casting.

The crevalle jack is usually on the prowl, singly, in small packs or in schools. When it is feeding, so fast is its plunging pursuit of food fish that anything tossed at it—spoon, feather, squid, plug, streamer, fish strip—will result in a jolting strike. If the first jack misses, another will be in on the lure almost immediately.

They should be fished with light tackle, but not because they need any handicaps. The crevalle jack charges into as rough a go-round, once pricked by a hook, as almost any fish in Florida waters. Their strike is so savage they either hook themselves or are on their way before the angler can do too much about it. Their first run is strong and vicious, and a fisherman should use the utmost care to see that no improper tensions or slack of line are permitted.

There are times when crevalle will pick up a bottom bait. But best results can be obtained, when an angler is in areas frequented by jack, by keeping a constant lookout for their surface feeding and running and by being ready for their approach with artificial lures.

Edibility

Fair, if they are bled immediately on removing from water. Taste can be improved by placing in heavily salted water 45 minutes before cooking.

Weights

Florida record: 38 lbs. School average: 2 - 3 lbs. Pack average: 5 - 15 lbs.

Jack, Horse-Eye

Caranx latus
HORSE-EYE JACK

Identification

The horse-eye jack has a grayish-blue back with a sharply defined vertical line and pronounced bony scutes. The eye is deep brown, especially large and luminous. The darker back shades to golden and silver sides. Tailfin is yellow. Shape identical with the crevalle jack, but unlike the crevalle, the chest shows a covering of small scales.

Location

The horse-eye jack shows up chiefly in southern Florida waters, but it is not nearly as common as the crevalle jack, and seems to prefer deeper water, reefs and the Gulf Stream edge. It is sometimes taken, however, by bridge fishermen fishing channels on the Keys, the area in which it is most numerous.

Methods of Fishing, Habits

Best methods are trolling, plug casting.

They rush feathers, plugs, spoons or trolled strips, following the general habits of the crevalle. Over outer reefs, light tackle can be enjoyably used when a small school or group is located. Their strike is hard, with furious yanking runs following.

Edibility

Not to be eaten. There seems definite evidence that a certain type of fish poisoning results from consumption of the flesh. They are often banned from commercial sale.

Weights

Taken on light tackle up to 15 lbs. Reported to 25 lbs.

Jack, Yellow

Caranx bartholomaei
BAR JACK, YELLOW JACK

Identification

Color is a silvery blue with a golden sheen. The fins are a light yellow. Unlike the crevalle, it has no black spot on the gill covers. A purple stripe traces the back outline above the lateral line.

Location

South Florida area. Taken on outer reefs, in waters deeper than those preferred by crevalle jack. Often found with amberjack.

Methods of Fishing, Habits

Fights and feeds similarly to other members of the jack family. Has a preference for bright spoons and metal squids. It is an incidentally caught fish, taken usually when trolling for amberjack.

Edibility

Only fair.

Weights

Florida average: 3 - 4 lbs. Goes to 15.

Florida Gamefish

Jewfish, Black

Garrupa nigrita

WARSAW GROUPER, JEWFISH

Identification

The second largest member of the grouper family, exceeded in size only by the spotted jewfish.

It is black in color with dark patchy gray markings. Mouth is enormous and general shape follows closely that of the spotted jewfish and other groupers.

Location

The black jewfish is more of a deep-water fish than its close relative, the spotted jewfish, and is seldom located in inshore waters. It feeds over the outer reefs and coral formations, is most frequently taken during the late spring and summer months. It is found in all Florida waters.

Methods of Fishing, Habits

Best methods are still fishing over outer reefs with large live or cut baits; drifting.

Hooking into a Warsaw grouper is not unlike hooking bottom or a slow, down-moving elevator. Time should be given the fish to swallow the bait, and once the hook is set, careful judgment should be used to determine the weight of the fish before attempting to horse or lift too rapidly. The fight is a slow dogged pull, the fish attempting to sound or reach the safety of rocks.

Edibility

Good.

Weights

Florida average: 25 lbs. 150-200 lb. catches fairly frequent in summer months. Reported to 500 lbs.

Jewfish, Spotted

Promicrops itaiara

JEWFISH, BLACK SEA BASS

Identification

The giant of Florida waters. It's the largest of the grouper family, going to more than 600 lbs. in weight. Bright spots and mottlings are evident in smaller specimens, fade out in the larger, which are a dull patchy blackish-brown all over. The mouth is enormous.

Location

All Florida waters, most numerous in southern parts and on the Keys. It is found in holes around bridge pilings and banks heavy with mangrove growth. Large specimens inhabit reefs. It can generally be considered that the Keys area produces the largest fish. Occasionally frequent in lower Gulf Coast waters in weights approximately 25 lbs.

Methods of Fishing, Habits

Best method is still fishing with the heaviest possible tackle.

The ponderous jewfish is no respecter of tackle. This specimen weighed 225 pounds. The spotted variety, largest of the grouper family, reaches the massive weight of 600 pounds.

Most anglers in quest of jewfish set a tarred ⅝ in. rope to which is appended a link-chain leader and 12/0 hand-forged hook in a hole where jewfish have been previously sighted. The fish is usually a "permanent resident" of its selected feeding-ground.

The fish mouths or slowly gulps its bait and time should be allowed before setting the hook. Whole mullet and large grunts are surest baits. The fish is sluggish but determined, and taking one puts the angler and fish in the division of the grunt-and-groan school of wrestlers. Even the heaviest of tackle will give under the terrific weight and dogged pull of the jewfish and patience should be exercised in lifting the fish from its hole.

It has been noted the jewfish will take a slow-trolled lure — the largest plugs, spoons. This method has little merit, considering the weight of the fish and the tackle necessary to play is successfully.

Edibility

Once thrown away, the jewfish is now known to be a fine delicacy properly steaked. Possibly first considered so many years ago by Key Westers, who learned to appreciate the fine-grained, white, succulent flesh.

Weights

Average: 150 - 300 lbs. To 600 lbs.

Florida Gamefish

Ladyfish

Elops sauris

LADYFISH, CHIRO

Identification

The name "Ten-pounder," used in many reference works, is a complete misnomer for this game, slender fighter, which seldom exceeds 2 to 3 pounds in weight, averaging 1 to 1½ pounds. In Florida the term "ladyfish" is common and widely accepted, while "chiro" is used in some East Coast fishing centers. Fishermen unfamiliar with subtropical waters sometimes also mistake the ladyfish for a bonefish, although even a hasty glance at their characteristics show the wide differences between the two.

The ladyfish is a slender, silvery fish with small scales, light green back, pointed head and large jaws in contrast to the more dazling silver, heavy scales and comparatively small mouth of the bonefish. The ladyfish takes to the air immediately on being hooked, while the bonefish never leaves the water.

Location

Greatest concentrations are found along the Gulf Coast the year-round, in considerable quantity along Atlantic beaches and inlets. The ladyfish is, for all practical purposes, to be considered a shoreline, bay and inlet fish and is fished, especially on the Gulf, wading or casting from beaches or at inlets.

Methods of Fishing,

Habits

Best methods are light-tackle casting, trolling.

The ladyfish is an active, running fighter that shows little preference when on the prowl, taking almost any lure that moves—small or moderate size—feather, plug, the regular spinning lures, spoons. It will also pick up cut baits and rush with lightning rapidity to start surface fighting.

The action is furious, a ladyfish almost always taking to the air and staying there in a whipping, slashing attempt to free itself. Probably no saltwater fish, if hooked on very light tackle, spends as much time out of the water as does this thin, wiry battler. They feed at night as well or better than in the day. An angler cannot make his retrieve too speedy for a ladyfish with its fast, charging strike.

Edibility

Flesh is good, but because of the extremely numerous bones anglers usually pass them up in favor of more easily prepared table fish. Recipes for shad can be followed.

Weights

Record: no acceptable Florida record. In neighborhood of 8 lbs. Average: 1 - 1½ lbs.

Mackerel, Cero

Scomberomourous regalis

CERO MACKEREL, CERO, PAINTED MACKEREL

Identification

A continuous gold line runs the length of the body, with three or four broken parallel lines formed by a succession of narrow oblong markings of gold and golden brown. The continuous vertical line is usually centered.

The body is light blue on the back, and sides are silvery-white. Scales are small, as are the pointed, pin-sharp teeth.

The cero has long been confused in name with both Spanish mackerel and king mackerel, the cero designated in some parts of Florida by the more apt term "painted mackerel." Common usage in recent years now makes employment of the term "cero" essential in differentiating it from the larger green-and-silver king mackerel and the distinctly marked Spanish mackerel.

Location

The cero, a year-round resident of south Florida areas, especially in the lower Keys, shows in considerable numbers along the lower Florida coasts in the spring and summer months. It is usually found on outer reefs and at the edge of the Gulf Stream.

Methods of Fishing,

Habits

Best method is trolling with feathers, strips appended.

Cero are often taken while trolling with heavy gear for larger fish, their excellent fighting abilities thus minimized. They should be fished with lightweight tackle, small white and yellow metal-headed feathers with short mullet or bonito strips appended. Light-weight wire leader should be exceptionally long for cero as for other mackerels, both for deception and to prevent line-cutting from the sharp-toothed jaws. Its fight, strike and run follow in nature that of the Spanish mackerel, but it is generally more dogged.

Edibility

Excellent. A fine white flesh, not quite as oily as the Spanish mackerel, lighter in color than the king mackerel.

Weights

Florida average: 3 lbs. Reported to 25 lbs.

Florida Gamefish

Looking over their catch of King Mackerel, these boys felt satisfied with their afternoon's efforts. They had a 150-pound Jewfish and several Cobia to go with the Kings and a couple of Barracuda. They trolled with a Reflecto Spoon, around an offshore beacon.

Mackerel, King

Scomberomorous cavalla

KINGFISH, KING, KING MACKEREL

Identification

The long, sleek-skinned king flashes an over-all green and silver iridescence, tarnished silver sides, and is void of spots, except at the smallest stages. It is a far larger fish than either the related Spanish mackerel or cero, and should not be confused with the yellow dotted and striped cero, although the misnomer "cero" was once widely applied. The single word "kingfish" is probably the most commonly used Florida term today.

Location

Migrations follow the Spanish mackerel schools, vast numbers massing in winter months in the Straits of Florida before beginning their runs northward along both Florida coasts. During spring migrations especially, fishermen off Fort Myers, St. Petersburg, Clearwater and further up the Gulf Coast claim they have the heaviest concentrations to be found. In summer months the upper East Coast is a rich grounds. Fall finds the fish moving back southward and the Keys get a good play during this period. Stragglers are caught all year-round.

Kings are a deep-water fish, taken in and near the Stream, over outer reefs, in offshore Gulf waters.

Methods of Fishing, Habits

Best methods are trolling. Fished with natural baits and lures on light tackle during runs on Gulf Coast.

The king has a fast, electrifying strike. They seem to be always on the move, with the throttle wide open, smashing and cutting at baits with great speed and force.

Their favorite natural foods are balao and small mullet. Metal-headed feather lures with a small mullet strip for a streamer—too great a length of the strip will result in the fast-charging kings missing the hook area—are as good a lure as can be used. Commercial hook-and-line fishermen on the Gulf Coast don't bother with the slow method of natural baits, but prefer to use spoons, lead squids for fast hooking and unhooking. Wire leaders should always be 5 feet or more in length, to prevent the kings from cutting the line.

When fishing a big running school, the boat should make a forward progressive circle about a mile and a half in diameter, bisecting the circle on each go-round. This will keep the angler in the fast-cruising school of kings.

The fisherman should strike hard, always trying for instantaneous hooking, as kings come tearing in at the lures. If the strike is successful, the king often goes into aerial action, jumps up to 10 feet interspersed with long, oblique surface runs. The slightest slack, especially if using rigid-hook lead squids or spoons, will free the fish.

During known runs, if kings are not showing or striking near the surface, weighted trolls on wire lines are put into use. This method obviously limits the fighting action of the fish, with the weights necessary to get baits down to the depth of the fish going to a half-pound of lead, but it is remunerative and widely employed by commercial fishermen.

Edibility

Excellent. Flesh firm, tasty. Preparation easy. After gutting (fish is scaleless), slice like a loaf of bread, broil or pan fry.

Weights

World record: 76½ lbs. Florida average: schools, 5 - 8 lbs., solitary to 40 lbs.

Mackerel, Spanish

Scomberomorus maculatus

SPANISH MACKEREL

Identification

A handsome silvery-sided and silver-bellied fish with brilliant large gold dots on the sides. The back is greenish-blue, the mouth fairly large with fine needle-sharp teeth. Front dorsal is high, higher than that of the cero or king and is black in color.

A string of Mackerel (Spanish Mackerel) such as this is a common sight on the docks of most any Florida seaside community. They run in schools, in countless numbers and will strike a trolled metal spoon (best liked is the No. 1 Clarkspoon). Sometimes croaker and Whiting are picked up with the trolled lures, such as these fishermen are displaying over their Mackerel string.

Florida Gamefish

Location

All Florida waters. The Spanish mackerel schools in great numbers, moving down both Florida coasts in October. In early April they start northern migrations along the shorelines, and April, May and early June are especially rewarding months for the angler fishing inshore waters. Although the months noted are those when Spanish mackerel are most numerous, they are caught casually the year-round, especially in the more southerly Florida areas.

During migrations, great numbers are taken along beaches, at river mouths and in backwater bays, from bridges and small skiffs.

Methods of Fishing, Habits

Best methods are trolling, light-tackle casting.

During migration periods, the often vast schools reveal themselves most obviously by their water-chopping surface feeding, and the almost inevitable convoy of wheeling, screaming gulls overhead.

Trolling with feathers or strips in offshore water, using a leader approximately six feet in length, will bring mackerel moving below the surface into action. Once a school is sighted, casting or spinning gear can be used with fine rewards of fish and sport. Almost any moving lure—weighted feathers, tin squids, bucktails, small spoons—will spur the mackerel to their sharp, slashing strikes. It's far better, once in the middle of a school, to discard time-wasting strip baits, so rapid is the action.

The mackerel makes a pouncing, snapping strike, following it immediately with short but powerful runs. For its weight, it is a hard-fighting fish. Its rapid moving in on trolled baits provides an annoyance to anglers seeking larger fish because of its habit of hitting strips well to the rear, out of the hook area.

For skiff-, bay-, bridge, and dock-fishing during mackerel runs, live bait and shrimp are used in still fishing. It is recommended that a second rod equipped with tin squid, feather or spoon be handy for the cruising pods or schools that may move rapidly into—and out of—the vicinity of the stationary fisherman.

Edibility

A widely-favored table fish. Easy to fillet. Spanish mackerel, however, spoils fairly quickly, and on all-day trips in high temperatures they should be iced as soon as caught.

Weights

Florida average: 2-2½ lbs. 4 lbs. not unusual. Reported to 18 lbs.

Marlin, Blue

Makaira ampla
BLUE MARLIN

Identification

Blue marlin are massive-bodied, the continuous dorsal and back a deep blue in color, shading to silver sides and belly. Blue-lavender vertical stripes flush brightly when the fish is aroused to strike or when hooked, fade rapidly when once out of the water. The bill is cylindrical, similar to that of the sailfish, but stubbier, thicker, more dagger- than rapier-like.

Location

The blue marlin is not a common fish on the west side of the Gulf Stream. Their range, for the Florida fisherman, can be said to be well out in the Stream from the Palm Beaches south. They are far more numerous on the eastern side of the Stream, to which charters (expensive) from East Coast centers, can be arranged to fish nearby Bahama waters, especially the Cat-Cay-Bimini areas.

Methods of Fishing, Habits

Best method is trolling with heavy gear.

Blue marlin follow the pattern of the other speared fish, striking their prey with their bills in an effort to stun or kill before swallowing. Thus the delayed striking technique is employed, throwing the reel to release when the tapping strike is felt, permitting the bait to idle and begin to sink. Knowing anglers do not permit as much time to elapse from the moment of the tap by the marlin to the attempted setting of the hook as they allow a sailfish.

The blue marlin is fiercely aggressive, surging upward with great speed to stun and gorge his prey. The first run on hooking is a searing, line-ripping charge seaward that threatens destruction of the tackle and freedom for the fish. This is quickly followed by an awesome aerial exhibition of incredible jumps, tail-walking in a shower of frothing spray across the surface, unexpected dives and soundings. Their strength seems inexhaustible, their change of pace so bewildering that the slightest laxity on the part of the angler may mean a loss of the fish.

Baits are fashioned similarly to those used for sail, except they must be far larger. Best bait is a 3- to 4-lb. bonefish, threaded, with the back broken or backbone removed so it will show a natural motion. Trolling is very rapid, the bait skipping along the surface. Very large mullet, 4 lb. dolphin or mackerel are also used.

The experienced crews that charter for marlin supply both the know-how and the heavy, expensive tackle necessary for successfully taking the great speared fish.

Edibility

Good. A commercial fish in Cuba.

Weights

World record (rod and reel): 796 lbs. Florida average: 300 lbs.

Blue Marlin, rated as aristocrats of the deep, are rarely found west of the Gulf Stream. So, when the mighty gamester shown above was taken by these vacationers in front of the Tides Hotel in St. Petersburg, it was rated as a fantastic fishing experience for the Gulf of Mexico. The Marlin was a perfect specimen and fought to the last gasp.

Marlin, White

Makaira albida
WHITE MARLIN

Identification

This superb game fish is in many ways a miniature of the great blue marlin. The back is a deep blue, upper portions of the silvery sides latticed with regularly spaced vertical markings.

The front of the dorsal is distinctly rounded, in contrast to the scimitar-shaped dorsal of the blue marlin. The tail is the wide forked tail of both the sailfish and the blue marlin.

Location

White marlin are most frequently found in Florida waters from Stuart south and are often taken by anglers in search of sailfish. They course the Gulf Stream in the manner of sailfish, but are less numerous, the reverse being true across the Stream in Bahamian waters, where white marlin outnumber sailfish. They are seasonal in their appearance, regular catches in Florida beginning in February, with the best months April, May and early June.

Methods of Fishing, Habits

Best method is trolling. Baits, tackle the same as sailfish—threaded mullet, balao, strips.

The white marlin offers the angler about everything he could wish to meet in wariness, power and agility. It has a habit of rising from the depths to pursue a fast-trolled bait for hundreds of yards in a most tantalizing fashion, putting the angler on edge with tense expectancy. A change of boat speed or a sudden decision by the fish that he likes the looks of what he's following, brings the exciting tap on the line. Following the moments allowed by delayed striking technique comes a free-for-all of scorching runs and frenzied leaps, rapid reversals of direction and plunges into the air for tail-walks across the sea, the marlin's spike angrily flailing the air.

White marlin average as much as 30 pounds heavier than the similarly performing sailfish. Experienced anglers confine themselves to the use of moderately light tackle to give this magnificent fish an apportunity to display its full dramatic fighting powers, lines testing 27 pounds most common. Heavier tackle is recommended for the inexperienced angler.

Edibility

Should be released when not desired for mounting or as a citation fish.

Weights

Florida-world Record (Miami Beach): 161 lbs. Florida average: 60 lbs.

Florida Gamefish

Mullet

Mugil cephalus

MULLET

Mullet will be encountered everywhere by the visiting angler, this valuable food and bait fish inhabiting Florida waters in vast numbers.

A tall tale of Audubon's day relates that tremendous mullet schools "impeded the progress of his boat" somewhere in the Jacksonville-St. Augustine area. It is not too incredible. Despite the wanton slaughter of earlier years, good state conservation measures and a public conscience have now combined to give this valuable fish some much-needed protection.

Mullet invade bays and rivers and move in dense schools along shorelines, evidencing their presence by circular whorls on the water's surface and endless stiff-bodied aerial leapings. Just why they jump so regularly and constantly is still a matter of conjecture, including theories they are freeing themselves from clinging parasites, that they seek the air's oxygen, that they are feeding on small insects. No satisfying answer to their jumping habits has yet appeared.

It is simple for the angler, once he has watched a circling school or pod of mullet, to differentiate them from other surface-working fish by their characteristic leapings. They take to the air with a forward jump, head skyward, body seemingly rigid as they reach the apex of their jump. Then they fall straight and stiff back into the water, their tails making a fluttering noise as they disappear.

Mullet is the most widely used bait in Florida, as all game fish seek mullet as food. Small live mullet are choice bait for tarpon and many other large game fish and mullet is most widely used as trolled bait for the big gamesters of the Gulf Stream. The mullet is not carnivorous, will not strike baits, feeds chiefly on vegetable matter. The fish itself is silver-sided, with faint to pronounced stripelike lateral markings, the mouth small, the back a dusky blue to black. The flesh of the mullet is good, white and tasty. Mullet roe, in the Gulf Coast and mid-Atlantic areas, is considered a delicacy, and the "bank-loafers"—mullet going to four pounds netted along banks of bays and rivers—are considered a choice table fish by many local residents.

Permit

Trachinotus goodei

PERMIT

Identification

The back of the permit is a deep to a bright blue, occasionally showing a sea-green cast, the sides are silvery and the belly is tinged with yellow. The tail is deeply forked, the body follows the outlines of the pompano. In earlier years the permit was often referred to as the great or the Mexican pompano, terms no longer used by Florida fishermen.

Anglers fortunate enough to hook one of these rare, prized fish can further differentiate the permit from the pompano by its far greater size, its locale and habits as noted below.

Location

The permit can be considered a shallow-water fish, an inhabitant of flats and holes adjacent to sandy or grassy flats. Its locales are south of Tarpon Springs on the Gulf, it is occasionally in the Indian River country, more plentiful in the Keys, although the permit is not a frequent fish in any area. They are occasionally taken in channels and passes, in deep holes under bridges, but the meager data available on their location and habits indicate that when permit are found in deeper waters they are moving to feed on flats and shoals.

Methods of Fishing, Habits

Best method is still fishing, medium-heavy tackle, with hermit crab, crawfish, live shrimp.

Anglers expert in the art of bonefishing sometimes speak admiringly of the permit as its "heavyweight brother" because of the general similarity of feeding habits and locale, its skittishness and its powerful, torpedo-straight runs, once hooked.

No data exists that pinpoints the exact location of permit, their common feeding times or their habits. It can be said permit are far more often seen than caught, many experienced Keys fishermen having fished year after year without bringing one to gaff.

When permit are moving over flats, they feed in bonefish fashion, stirring up mud and sand whorls. At such times, carefully placed casts well ahead of the fish may result in a strike, the greatest care must be exercised, however, to prevent alarming them to sudden flight. In channels, inlets and holes under bridges on the Keys where they congregate, permit seem to pause for an hour or so to feed on mid-flood tides. At these times they should be still-fished on the bottom with sound tackle, as runs are fierce and long and permit rush to shear off lines against pilings and abutments with disheartening regularity.

Light tackle is not recommended except for the most expert angler with an unlimited amount of time. Guides can be located in the middle Keys area who are familiar with the vast flats and shallow reaches of their locale; these are the best bet for the ambitious angler seeking to tangle with the fish declared by those who have caught them to be "the roughest fighting shallow-water fish in the world."

Edibility

Excellent. A delicacy.

Weights

World-Florida record: 42¼ lbs. Reported to 60 lbs. Florida average: 10-25 lbs.

Pompano, African

Synnis bubensis

AFRICAN POMPANO

Identification

The African pompano follows the jacks in general body outline, differentiated by a somewhat steeper profile and long feathery spines trailing off from the upper dorsal. It is a handsome fish, made especially so by the silver-toned iridescence gleaming over the light blue tones of the body. Large bony scutes protrude from the lateral line on the tail-section.

Location

For all practical purposes the African pompano confines its appearance to south Florida waters, its greatest frequency being during the spring and summer months. It is a comparatively scarce fish, usually taken while fishing amberjack and other reef fish.

Methods of Fishing, Habits

Best method is trolling over reef waters.

African pompano are generally caught incidentally on strip and other baits while trolling for reef fish. They are occasionally taken in channels and cuts by anglers using live shrimp, but this is not common.

The strike is comparable to that of the crevalle jack, followed by a series of hard, jolting runs.

Edibility

Poor. Should be released when not desired for mounting.

Weights

No established record. To 30 lbs. in Florida tournaments. Reported to 37 lbs. Average 10 lbs.

Pompano, Common

Trachinotus carolinus

POMPANO

Identification

The pompano is wide-sided, its back a gray-blue, its belly yellow-tinted, with the upper fins dark and the lower fins yellowish. There is a blue patch just above the eye and the sides show a silvery sheen. The yellowish tail is deeply forked.

A world record Pompano, caught on the beach with an ordinary rod and reel and a piece of shrimp. The exploits of surf and shore fishermen-and-women are legion and sometimes unbelievable.

Location

Pompano are found in all Florida waters. They course the beaches in the surf, feed in inlets and at river mouths. Although taken in some quantity on the East Coast, especially in mid-state areas, their frequency is greatest along the entire length of the Gulf Coast. They swim and feed in small schools in the low surf of the Gulf beaches, ordinarily confining themselves to sandy bottoms.

Methods of Fishing, Habits

Best methods are surf-fishing with shrimp and sand fleas, light-tackle casting with small nylon jigs on bottom or with slow, weighted troll.

The pompano is an eagerly sought fish by light-tackle anglers for its strong running fight, its wariness and its great-touted excellence as one of the finest of all fish for the table. Until recently, pompano were almost exclusively fished with sand fleas and shrimp, but Gulf Coast fishermen found that by using small artificials — preferably white or yellow nylon jigs on spinning or bait-casting rods—and permitting the lure to sink to the sandy bottom and then lifting the jig with a sharp motion for a distance of a foot or so, pompano strike with even greater alacrity than they do on natural baits. Some Gulf Coast pompano fishermen claim a three to one return over the old manner of still fishing with sand fleas and shrimp by employing this method.

Further, a slow troll over sand close inshore which allows the weighted lure to bounce along the bottom, will bring pompano into action.

The pompano strike is hard and fast. Its fight is similar to that of a tripletail, twisting its body sidewise to create added resistance. Spring and summer months are the most productive.

Edibility

A prized gourmet dish. It brings the highest price of any fish in Florida, is considered by many to be unequaled in its piquant flavor and fine-textured flesh.

Weights

Florida average: 1½ lbs. Often to 3 lbs. Reported to 8 lbs.

Pompano, Round

Trachinotus falcatus
ROUND POMPANO

Identification

Usually confused with common pompano.

The round pompano's distinguishing characteristics are a more rounded form and an absence of the golden sheen noticeable on common pompano. Some good authorities claim the fish is a young permit, but its rounder shape and steeper profile and slightly larger dorsal lobes dispute such a claim.

Location

South Florida waters. Seldom found above Fort Pierce or Tampa. They feed in shallow shore and bay waters, often over sandy bottoms. If a round pompano is caught it is an indication that a school of common pompano is nearby, as they feed and move with their close relatives. The round pompano is scarce enough that they are never fished for exclusively.

Methods of Fishing, Habits

Follow the methods noted under pompano.

Edibility

Comparable but not quite up to pompano.

Weights

No record. 3 lbs. about top. Average: 1 lb.

Porgies

Porgy, Grass

Calamus arctifrons
GRASS PORGY

The grass porgy is the brightest and most colorful of the porgies. A yellow patch marks the nose, the sides are a dark barred gray-green, and the fins show a bluish cast. Like all porgies, it is a high-profiled fish, and its weight is usually in the pound division. It feeds over grassy bottoms, as its name implies. It is found most frequently on the Gulf Coast and is especially plentiful in the Tampa-Clearwater area.

Porgy, Jolt-Head

Calamus bajonade
JOLT-HEAD

The jolt-head has a dull metallic-colored back, darkish fins and an exceptionally high forehead. Its range includes the lower portions of the East Coast, the Keys and Florida Bay. It feeds over shell and sandy bottoms.

Porgy, Little-Head

Calamus proridens
LITTLE-HEAD PORGY

The little-head porgy approaches the grass porgy in its brilliance of coloration. Its range and feeding bottoms follow mainly those of the jolt-head. It is caught in some numbers on the lower Gulf Coast.

Porgy, Southern

Stenotomus aculeatus
PORGY

The southern porgy is fairly common over all the Florida coasts. On the upper East Coast from St. Augustine to Fernandina they are especially plentiful and are usually found feeding over hard shell bottoms. In appearance it is the same as the porgy caught in such numbers in North Carolina at Pamlico Sound and off Morehead City. It is not quite as steep-profiled as the grass porgy, has faint rust-brown barrings over green and gray upper sides and a light mottled tail. Its belly is silvery.

Edibility

Porgies are a prime pan fish. They are widely used commercially and are sought by sports anglers, using the lightest tackle, as a fish that will put up a good little scrap for its weight and make a tasty dish at the end of the day. The flesh is very white and well-flavored. Porgies are eager feeders on shrimp, especially live ones. Small baits of blue claw and hermit crab run next in favor.

Weights

The weights of all the porgies range from ½ lb. to 1 lb., going rarely to 2 lbs.

Florida Gamefish

Shark hunting clubs have sprung up all along Florida's coasts. There is no more dedicated fisherman than the "shark fighter" once he has been bitten by the bug. The specimen shown above has been identified as an adult blacknose shark. A key identification feature is its pointed snout. In young specimens, the snout is darker.

Rays

Ray, Manta

Manta birostis

The most spectacular ray is the giant of the ocean, the manta ray, commonly referred to as the devilfish. This great bargelike fish reaches a span of more than 20 feet from tip to tip of its huge batlike "wings" and a weight of more than 3,000 lbs.

Mantas are often found floating seemingly motionless on the surface of shoal waters, appearing dark and ominous in the sun like some strange, anchored raft. Throwing a harpoon into the broad back of a manta sets off a thunderous explosion of water-churning fury as the ray charges seaward with an incredible surge of power. A second and a third harpoon are usually necessary to check and hold the streaking fish, and so great is their strength it is not unusual for a good-sized cabincruiser to be towed for two or three hours before the manta shows signs of weakening.

In their flailing flight, manta take to the air in tremendous skyward thrusts, falling back with a thunderous smack on the water's surface. Their speed of movement is rapid, using their wing tips in a birdlike motion—beating and churning when under attack, graceful and undulating when free-swimming.

Florida Gamefish

Ray, Spotted Eagle

Myliobatus freminvillei

The colorful, spotted eagle ray, blackish and heavily dotted with white, is a fairly common sight, especially in Keys waters. Eagle rays have a propensity to travel in pairs, will take almost any natural bait and give anglers a tough time in shallow water, making long runs and often taking to the air to throw a hook.

Ray, Sting

Dasyatis say

The sting ray is the most common of the rays, an annoying feeder for bottom- fishermen and a somewhat dangerous lurker on flats for wading anglers. A bony barb on the tail is covered with an infectious slime, and the wound on the leg of an unwary wader can be painful and lasting. Cutting the line is probably the safest and most economical method to follow when hooking one of the larger specimens.

Runner, Blue

Caranx crysos

BLUE RUNNER

Identication

The back of the blue runner is a light greenish-blue, the lower sides silvery, shading to a creamy yellow belly. It is somewhat more slender and lighter-bodied than the crevalle jack.

Location

All Florida waters, bays, inlets and shorelines preferred, especially by smaller specimens found in large schools.

Methods of Fishing, Habits

Best methods are casting, trolling, fly-rod fishing.

The blue runner is a bantam-weight champion, going into fine frenzied action on almost any bait offered, especially when located in the large schools in which it moves along shorelines and into bays and inlets. On incoming tides over flats, bottom baits will be quickly picked up, but inasmuch as the runner is an aggressive and easily-pleased striker, small artificials offer the best sport.

Edibility

Only fair, comparable to crevalle.

Weights

Average: 1 lb. Up to 5 lbs.

Runner, Rainbow

Elagatis binpinnulatus

RAINBOW RUNNER

Identification

A most infrequently caught member of the jack family. The back and upper sides are blue, the lower sides are yellow and marked with a light blue stripe. Fins are brilliant yellow. Both dorsal and anal fins appear interrupted near tail with a smaller additional fin.

Location

Stream and outer reefs, usually from Miami south.

Methods of Fishing, Habits

Best method is trolling.

Not individually sought, they are taken while trolling the Gulf Stream or outer reefs for other fish. Thus their hard fight is minimized by the use of heavy tackle.

Edibility

Good to excellent.

Weights

Averag: 3 lbs. Reported to 15 lbs.

Sailfish, Atlantic

Istiophorus americanus

SAILFISH, SAIL

Identification

The body of the sailfish is as slender and graceful as the fish is spectacular in action. The bill, or spear, is rapierlike, the vivid deep blue dorsal that accounts for the term "sail"

Sailfish are a top gamefish anywhere you see a fleet of charter boats on the Atlantic coast of Florida. In recent years the Gulf of Mexico has become populated by Sails and the sport is fast taking over many formerly happy Tarpon fishermen. This excited Gulfport girl caught her Sailfish just a short run offshore from Pass-a-Grille, near St. Petersburg.

is exceptionally large, sprinkled with faint black polkadot markings. The tail is deeply forked. When the sail is folded or down, it rests in a slotlike indentation on the back.

The contrast of the ink-blue back, high flaring dorsal and burnished silver lower sides, gives the sailfish a strikingly handsome appearance. Under stress of attack, dark latticing vertical stripes formed from closely spaced dots come to view on the back and upper sides, the silvers and blues intensifying.

Location

The Atlantic sail can be justly claimed as Florida's own most highly prized great game fish of the blue waters. Sail are found the length of Florida's Atlantic Coast, usually in or at the edge of the Gulf Stream.

Good catches are made from East Coast ports — Fort Pierce, Fort Lauderdale, Pompano Beach, Miami and towns along the Keys to Key West. However, records support the claims of anglers in the Stuart-Palm Beach areas that sail are more numerous in this stretch of waters, where the Gulf Stream swings so close to shore, than at any point in Florida.

It should be noted that during the late fall months, with few anglers on hand to meet them, large concentrations of sail appear along the Keys. At that time they may leave the Stream and move in over the reefs, where they can be sighted, slashing and cutting through schools of mullet and balao.

Currently, sailfish are being reported with some regularity far out in the wildernesses of Gulf waters. Inasmuch as few attempts are made by Gulf Coast anglers to fish sail,, sighted some 40 to 60 miles offshore, little data is available.

Methods of Fishing, Habits

Best methods are trolling with whole mullet, balao, mullet and bonito belly-strips.

Sailfish cruise speedily just below the surface of Gulf Stream waters in their search for food, racing through schools of smaller fish—pilchards, mullet, balao, flying fish—with flailing spears that stun and cripple their victims. The sail circle to inspect their hapless small prey before gorging. It was this habit of the billed fish that led to the development, in the 1920's, of the delayed-striking technique.

Baits are surface-trolled at rapid speeds offering a swift-swimming, skipping action. Threaded mullet have their backbone broken or a section removed to provide a natural undulation of the bait. Bonito belly-strips, preferred for their toughness and brightness, are carefully carved by the guides to provide an enticing fluttering.

If rods are fished on outriggers, the time-lapse, from the moment the line is jerked free of the clothespin by the tap of the sail's bill to the first moment the angler can set the hook, is about sufficient for the sail to make his decision whether or not to swallow the prey he believes he has stunned. If the rod is fished direct, without the use of an outrigger, on feeling the tap of the sail—more often than not the sailfish is easily visible in his pursuit along the water's surface—the release lever on the reel should be thrown instantly, permitting the bait and line to drop back for a slow count of ten. At the completion of this count, the angler makes a strong strike, trying to set the hook. If it is immediately clear that the fish has been missed, the angler should reel fast to attempt to lure the sail into making another tap.

To many fishermen this ten-second lapse is among the most thrilling moments an angler can experience. The sail may be seen weaving and turning, possibly with the sail half-erect, and a tense excitement takes hold as the tip of the rod is raised to come up on the fish and sink the hook.

Once the barb is set, the sailfish lunges skyward in a mighty leap, the spear wildly flailing. On sensing it has failed to free itself, it charges off across the sea in a series of plunges and fantastic tail-walkings, a wild melee that too often leaves the angler hopelessly watching a bellying line and the receding figure of the fish in great sprays of foam, diminishing with distance as the sail somersaults free of the hook.

Every effort is made by good sportsmen to promote the release of sailfish not desired for mounting or tournament credit. Release buttons, certificates of sportsmanship and citations are showered on visiting anglers who give sails their liberty, a gesture certainly deserved by the magnificent roaming performers of the Gulf Stream waters.

Edibility

Poor. Edible if smoked.

Weights

World record: 123 lbs. Florida average: 35 - 45 lbs.

A great confusion of terms identifying seatrout—or weakfish — has long persisted. Here the list and species will appear under seatrout, sand seatrout, silver seatrout and spotted seatrout, following the order of the Standard Check List.

Florida fishermen are prone to make either one or two general designations: "trout," including all four; or "trout" and "spotted seatrout," separately identifying only the spotted seatrout. Anglers used to northern waters often designate the lot as "weakfish" and "spotted weakfish," terms not used by Florida residents.

Seatrout

Cynoscion regalis

TROUT, SEATROUT

Identification

This is the weakfish of northern waters ("squeteague" in New England), with a light olive-green back and dark dots forming irregular oblique lines on the upper body. The tail is slightly indented rather than forked. The mouth is soft, and it is from this latter characteristic that the name "weakfish" is derived. The underbelly is light to white and the fins are yellowish.

Location

The seatrout is usually found only in the waters of the upper East Coast of Florida, making it the least common of the four salt-water trout caught in Florida. They school in ocean channels, inlets and shore waters.

Methods of Fishing, Habits

Best methods are bait-casting, surf-casting, still fishing with live shrimp and minnows. Will take cut bait fished on bottom.

Striking habits, fight and methods of taking seatrout follow generally those of the spotted seatrout, detailed below.

Edibility

Good.

Weights

World record: 17½ lbs. Florida average: 1 - 1½ lbs. To 5 lbs.

Seatrout, Sand

Cynoscion arenarius

SAND TROUT, TROUT

Identification

A very light-colored trout, with a somewhat darkish back, bright silver sides. The belly is silver-white. It is often hastily dubbed simply "seatrout," but the absence of dark dots and its much lighter color make it easy to differentiate it.

Location

The sand seatrout is found along the entire Gulf Coast of Florida. It feeds over sandy bottoms, along shorelines, in shallows of sandy bays.

Methods of Fishing, Habits

Best methods are bait-casting, with shrimp, cut mullet, minnows.

The sand seatrout follows the silver trout in its feeding. Although it is an avid bottom-feeder on crustacea and small minnows, it will take streamers and small feathers. Its fight, coming as it does in small sizes, is strong.

Edibility

Good.

Weights

No established record. Average: 1 lb. to 3½ lbs.

Seatrout, Silver

Cynoscion nothus

SILVER TROUT, TROUT

Identification

The smallest of the seatrout family. Tail rounded, no indentation. The back is a sea green, the sides and belly a bright silver. No dots or dark markings.

Location

Found in Florida chiefly on the Gulf Coast. It is a shore and bay fish, feeding over sand and grassy flats.

Methods of Fishing, Habits

Best methods are bait-casting, deep-fished streamers, still fishing with shrimp and cut bait.

The silver seatrout is a bottom-feeder, poking along over sand and grassy beds in search of shrimp and small minnows. It is, however, a hard-striking little fish and will take small artificials run well below the surface.

Edibility

Good.

Weights

Average: 1 lb. To 2½ lbs.

Seatrout, Spotted

Cynoscion nebulosus

SPOTTED TROUT, SPECKLED SEATROUT, SEATROUT

Identification

The speckled or spotted seatrout (the spotted weakfish of northern waters) is handsome in its coloration, the most brilliant of all the seatrout. Black dots pepper the upper sides and back, the second dorsal and the tail. The inside of the mouth is often yellowish, and the mouth is soft, tearing easily. The tail is squarish and slightly concave. The sides are silvery, the back, grayish to dark, with variations occurring according to the waters from which the fish is taken—darker over mud flats and in back bay waters, lighter in inlets and channels.

Location

The speckled trout has its greatest frequency in Florida waters, moving along beaches, ranging over grass flats and mud bottoms of bays and lagoons. It is found in quantity along the entire East Coast, is numerous in the back country of the Keys, across Florida Bay, is found frequently in rivers, bays and on grassy flats on the West Coast. In the vast inland bay known as the Indian River, the speckled trout reaches its peak in numbers and weight.

Methods of Fishing, Habits

Best methods are light-tackle casting with a wide choice of lures; still fishing with floated live bait and shrimp; "popcork" and splatter-pole fishing.

The speckled seatrout is a widely sought favorite of Florida anglers. It is a freely-striking fish, accepts a myriad number of artificials, almost every section of Florida preferring a special lure for its particular locale.

The feeding habits of the trout, taking the fish to banks lining lagoons, across flats and

Florida Gamefish

Spotted Seatrout, a most popular fish in Florida salt water is a handsome catch. This free-striking food fish is taken expertly with a pop cork and live shrimp, yet the variety of lures a Trout will grab is endless—and pure happiness to a rowboat fisherman.

over grassy beds, make them easily approached by foot. They can be fished as in fresh-water streams or from banks and docks. In the Indian River country, where there is somewhat of a purist approach to seatrout and where the trout are of an exceptional size, every angler propounds a certain method of his own as the one and only way of taking trout. These methods range from the use of a wide variety of spinning lures to a curious, pencil-shaped plug designed to dart along the surface, needlefish fashion. Many natural baits—live shrimp, live minnows, fingerling mullet—are also used at towns such as Cocoa, which calls itself the "Trout Capital of the World." From Titusville, through Cocoa, Melbourne and to Fort Pierce, trout averaging as much as six to eight pounds are commonplace, while in the Bay of Florida a four-pound trout is large.

The spotted seatrout is attracted by noise and from this habit "pop-cork" and splatter-pole fishing have developed. The pop cork is jerked to make a glubbing, gulping sound which imitates other surface-feeding fish. It seems to arouse the curiosity of nearby trout, bringing them to striking distance of the bait.

The splatter-pole is a long cane pole, equipped with a line about a foot longer than the pole itself. A bottle-cork or regular float is placed about three feet above the hook, which is usually baited with fingerling mullet. The pole is then slapped briskly on the water's surface, followed by a pause of a minute to await the strike of the inquiring trout.

Wise, speckled seatrout anglers are not too hasty in setting a hook with the strike of a trout, especially when using natural baits. The trout "mouths" a bait, and, once hooked, it should not be forced or horsed in the play, as hooks tear loose easily from the soft mouth.

The run and fight of a trout are strong, once it is hooked, and the trout will spend a lot of time surface-fighting. It does not, however, take to the air to free itself.

Edibility

Good to excellent. Flesh softens and deteriorates with long icing. Best during the cooler months.

Weights

World record: 15 lbs., 3 oz. Florida average (excluding central East Coast sector) to 3 lbs.

Florida Gamefish

Shad

Alosa sapidissima

SHAD

Identification

The back of the shad is a blue-green, the sides silvery. The fish is heavy-bellied and a black dot shows faint to bright on the gill cover. Dots are sometimes repeated along the sides.

Location

Not found with any frequency below the mouth of the St. Johns River and the Jacksonville area.

The shad seek fresh water for spawning, mysteriously disappearing to sea after completing their mission.

Methods of Fishing, Habits

For many years sports fishermen ignored the shad as a fish that would not take a hook, and shad were (and still are) chiefly taken by commercial netting methods.

Fly-fishermen experimenting during shad runs learned that the shad will strike a small bright spinner or spoon and streamer flies of various hues. These lures should always be allowed to sink. Slow trolling is also employed with success.

Shad should never be fished except when known runs are under way during the spawning season.

The shad offers a fine, water-frothing surface battle when hooked by light tackle.

The migration period for shad occurs during the late fall and early winter.

Edibility

Justly renowned. Shad roe is a gourmet delicacy. The usual cooking method is baking.

Weights

Undetermined. Reported to 13 lbs. Florida average: 3 - 4 lbs.

Sharks

The sharks noted here are only the more widely fished game sharks and some of those most commonly seen and caught in Florida waters. The list is by no means intended to be all-inclusive, some thirty varieties of sharks being found off the southern tip of Florida and along the Keys.

Anglers seeking sharks in the big-game division should equip themselves with extra-heavy tackle and, unless most experienced, employ guides to search out their quarry.

Shark, Great Black-Tipped

Carcharinus maculipinnis

Shark, Lesser Black-Tipped

Carcharhinus limbatus

BLACK-TIPPED SHARK, SPINNER SHARK

Identification

The great and lesser black-tipped sharks rank close to the mako and thresher sharks as fighting gamesters. Both lesser and great black-tipped sharks have black-stripe markings outlining their fins. These stripings are more evident in smaller and younger specimens.

An unusual characteristic of the black-tipped sharks is their curious twisting when jumping, their spins in the air sometimes numbering three or four complete revolutions in a single jump. This accounts for the common term applied to them by Florida fishermen—"spinner shark."

Location

They are fairly common on both Florida coasts, more widely fished in the Gulf. They strike large live baits and heavy cut baits offered around jetties and in offshore waters.

Weights

The great blacktipped shark is reported to go to 500 pounds, although few are seen above half that weight. The lesser black-tipped shark is chunkier in appearance but does not reach the weight of the great black-tipped shark, with 100 to 150 pounds the usual catch.

Shark, Hammerhead

Sphyrna zygaena

HAMMERHEAD SHARK

Identification

Hammerhead sharks, of which there are several closely related varieties (unimportant to the Florida angler), have a curious plow- or hammer-shaped, flattened head extending beyond the regular body outline. The hammerhead is common in Florida, picking up cut and live bait in bays and shallow water as well as in reef areas. Their fight is not overstrong.

Location

They are especially numerous in the waters of the Keys.

Edibility

The flesh is worthless.

Weights

The hammerhead goes to some 9 feet in length and 350 to 400 pounds in weight. Hammerheads are caught in Florida in all stages of growth, from 2-footers to those weighing several hundred pounds.

Florida Gamefish

Shark, Mako

Isurus glaucus

MAKO, MACKEREL SHARK

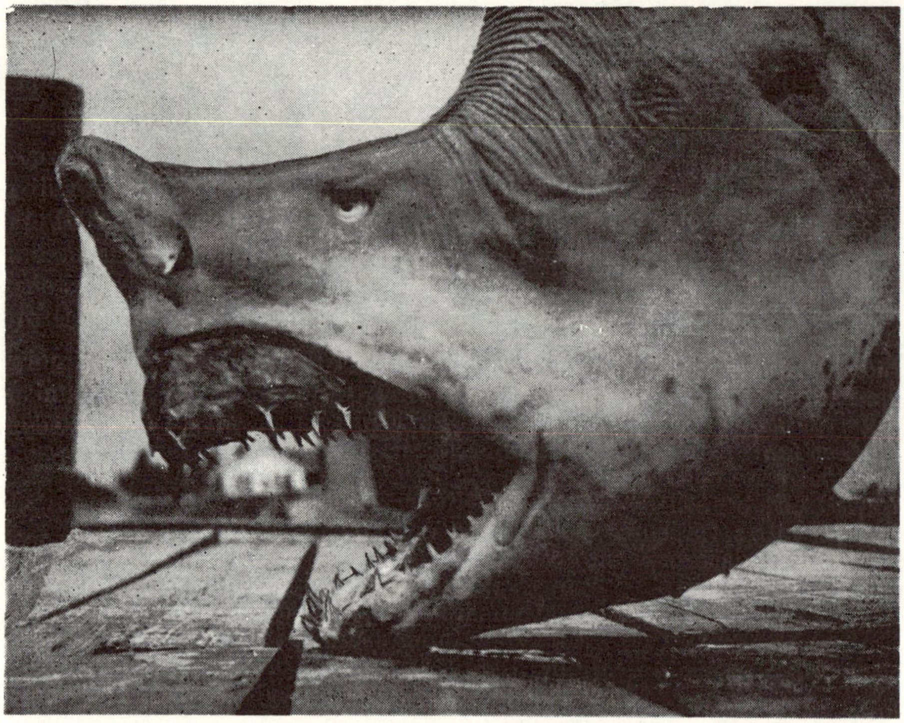

There are more than a score of shark varieties in Florida waters, all of them in the smaller sizes harmless to human beings. However, when any of the Blue Shark family attains a size of eight feet or larger, it is a potential man-eater and dangerous. The exception is the Nurse Shark which has no teeth. It can become a pet if kind treatment and good food are provided.

Identification

Long feared and avoided as much as possible by sports fishmen, some species of sharks have now been upgraded to the big game fish division by sportsmen who enjoy wrestling with overweight fighting fury for the sake of the spectacular combat. This is especially true of the mako, often called the mackerel shark. It is a fierce-striking shark which rushes from great depths to fight at the surface, matching the dramatic aerial performances of many of the most prized big game fish.

The mako can be called a handsome shark, with a sky-blue back and stark white underbelly. Its nose is sharp and pointed. Its runs are long and powered with tremendous strength. It will plunge skyward in a great shower of spray in a succession of frenzied jumpings. The fight at the boat's side is one that requires the most expert handling to avoid serious consequences from the huge snaggle-tooth jaws and the dangerous writhing and slapping body.

Location

It is found in all Florida areas, the larger specimens in deep offshore waters.

Edibility

It has been sampled as a tablefish and found pleasantly edible, excellent when smoked.

Weights

Makos go to 13 feet in length and 1,000 lbs. in weight. The world record is 1,000 lbs. and the Florida average ranges from 7 to 9 feet in length and from 200 to 400 pounds in weight.

Shark, Man-Eater

Carcharodon carcharias

MAN-EATER, WHITE SHARK

Identification

The heavier man-eater shark is not too often encountered. It is also designated as the white shark, or great white shark. The man-eater shark is most similar to the mako in its body outline, but goes to giant weights and a length of 15 feet is not unusual. The back of the man-eater is a gray-blue to almost black, with the sides and belly a muddy white. The teeth are large and jagged.

Location

Man-eaters usually range in deep waters. Swift-moving and savage, they are unquestionably the most dangerous shark in the sea and account for most of the hair-raising stories of their having devoured human flesh, although their comparative scarcity in Florida gives rise to some doubt of the truth of many of these legends. It is known, however, that they will voraciously devour huge turtles. In other areas their diet has been known to include everything from dogs to sea lions.

Anglers hooking a man-eater should exercise every caution. Reliable reports tell of hooked and harpooned man-eaters which, after vicious fighting, charged small boats like enraged bulls. They should be towed ashore, never boated in small craft, as they revive long after becoming seemingly lifeless and can create fatal havoc.

Weights

World record: 2,536 lbs.

Shark, Nurse

Ginglymostoma cirratum

NURSE SHARK

Identification

The nurse shark is easily tagged by a barbel hanging from the upper jaw, its yellow-rust color and what appears to be a single rudder-like upper portion of the tail fin. It moves chiefly in inshore waters, is in constant evidence in the Keys area and is taken on both coasts. Its fight is cowardly and unimpressive.

Weights

Nurse sharks have been reported over the 400-pound mark in Florida, with the average length 4 to 6 feet.

Shark, Thresher

Alopias vulpinus

THRESHER SHARK

Identification

The thresher shark is easily identified by the sickle-like, greatly extended upper portion of its tail fin. It is not as common as the mako off the Florida coasts. It is occasionally taken in upper Gulf Coast areas and is found most frequently in Florida Atlantic waters during the winter months. Old-timers in Florida always hasten to state that the thresher herds small fish into compact balls by using its long tail as a whip or a "thresher," then making a meal of its closely packed, terrified victims. The runs and furious jumpings of the thresher are close to those of the mako, though evidencing far less endurance.

Edibility

The flesh is sometimes sold commercially.

Weights

The world record for the thresher stands at 922 pounds, while 10- to 12-foot threshers are not unusual.

Shark, Tiger

Galeocerdo arcticus

TIGER SHARK, LEOPARD SHARK

Identification

The tiger shark is a dangerous killer, reported along with the man-eater as attacking human beings, although authenticated attacks are hard to track down. The upper body is blue, and vertical markings are faint to pronounced. The upper half of the tail is elongated and the nose is blunt.

Location

The tiger shark, especially numerous in the waters of the Keys, is found on both Florida coasts at river mouths, in bays and on shorelines as well as in deep waters. The fight of the tiger shark is strong and enduring.

Weights

Throughout the world the tiger shark goes to great lengths and weights, reported to 20 feet and some 1,400 pounds. In Florida waters 10- and 12-foot tiger sharks have been taken.

Sheepshead are a mainstay of the dock fisherman and beloved by all visitors who fish in Florida waters the easy way—with cane pole or hook and line. Many anglers use as bait the Fiddler Crabs found in such profusion scampering on the beaches. The "educated" Sheepshead fisherman has learned to use large barnacles or small oysters as bait—and to jerk the line *before the fish bites*. Practice and a rare sense of touch must be developed for success such as is evidenced in the picture above.

Sheepshead

Archosargus phobatocephalus

SHEEPSHEAD

Identification

A steep-profiled fish, easily recognized by its chunky body outline and sharply contrasting light and dark vertical bars, which, in younger and more brightly colored fish, create a prison-garb effect.

Location

The sheepshead is a year-round Florida inhabitant. There are large sheepshead in the Atlantic that are considered migratory, but sheepshead in the one- to four-pound class cluster around pilings, docks rocky shoals and bridge abutments with what can be called permanency. They are especially numerous on the Gulf Coast, where they school in the bay and shore areas, are scarce in the water of the Keys and on the lower East Coast.

Methods of Fishing, Habits

Best method is still fishing with fiddler crabs.

The sheepshead can qualify as being as tantalizing as the mangrove snapper in its suspicious approach to a hook. It takes a delicate nip at a bait with what seems to be only the forward part of the mouth. No time for guessing is permitted the angler, who must strike as concurrently as possible with the fast light nibble.

Where sheepshead are located in their drills around rock piles or pilings, chum of crushed fiddler crab will stir them into darting, competitive feeding most rewarding to the angler.

Edibility

Good. Should be skinned.

Weights

Florida average: 1, 1½ lbs. Reported to 25 lbs.

Snapper, Dog

Lutjanus jocu

DOG SNAPPER

Identification

The dog snapper is a deep-toned brownish-red. A short, irregular, broad line is scrawled beneath the eye. Light bar markings usually band the sides.

Location

The dog snapper is a deep-water inhabitant and is found only in the most southerly Florida areas. It is a fairly scarce fish, although at some seasons seems to appear in number on the Keys reefs.

Methods of Fishing, Habits

Taken incidentally while bottom fishing over reefs.

Edibility

Not eaten. The Bahamians' insistence that it is mildly poisonous has found wide acceptance among Florida residents.

Weights

Florida average: 3-4 lbs. Reported to 50 lbs.

Snapper, Lane

Lutjanus synagris

LANE SNAPPER, SPOT SNAPPER

Identification

A brilliantly-colored snapper, exceeded in beauty in its family only by the yellowtail. The lane snapper has bright pinkish tints coating the yellow body, a rosy tail, and a distinct black spot just below the back dorsal easily distinguishes the lane from other snapper. Yellow horizontal lines run the length of the body.

Location

Southern Florida. Most prolific in the waters of the Keys. They feed around pilings and docks, over inner reefs and sometimes on sand banks. Often found in company with mangrove snappers. Over inner reefs they gather in small packs of their own.

Methods of Fishing, Habits

Best methods are still fishing with crustaceans, cut bait.

Generally speaking, the methods used for taking mangrove snapper can be followed in pursuit of the lane snapper.

Edibility

Rates with the mangrove as a most tasty fish.

Weights

Record probably under 5 lbs. Average: ¾ - 1 lb.

Snapper, Mangrove

Lutjanus griseus

MANGROVE SNAPPER

Identification

Dark bandings mark the back of the mangrove snapper, the sides show reddish, varying in depth of hues according to the bottom over which it is caught. Over sand a light grayish tone replaces the pinks and reds of those caught on deep reefs or in darker bay and river waters. Dorsal and tail fins are usually dark, while pectoral and anal fins are pink-tinged.

Location

All Florida waters, most numerous in southern halves of Florida shorelines and through the Keys. It is found in big pods along the banks of mangrove islands, clusters around bridges and dock pilings and groups over both inner and outer reefs.

Methods of Fishing, Habits

Best methods are still fishing with cut bait, shrimp and crawfish, with smaller artificials, strip baits, streamers, worked deep on light tackle. Chumming is also very productive.

Florida fishermen hasten to award the mangrove snapper first prize as a most tantalizing fish. In the clear waters of the Keys they can be observed parading and drilling in numbers of 50 or more beneath a bridge or around a dock. They will churn the waters by rushing to snatch any desirable food dropped to them free of a hook. A similar bait lowered on a hook will bring snapper darting to within an inch of the rig, only to turn suspiciously away, making it almost an impossibility to hook them during sunlight hours. In disturbed or cloudy waters they strike more freely.

Chumming with broken bits of shrimp, crab or fish scraps is a fine method of starting mangrove-snapper feeding. As the snapper darts in for the feed, a hook similarly baited will bring good results.

A proven method in the clearer waters of South Florida and the Keys is to locate a good pod or school during the day and to begin fishing as the first powder of dusk darkens the waters. Sunset and the hour or two following are the most rewarding.

Over reefs and in deeper water, preferably using a monofilament line, the smartness of the mangrove snapper seems somewhat blunted, possibly by competition with other bottom fish for food and the greater depth.

The strike of the mangrove is a fast, flicking movement, and unless the hook is set instantaneously, the bait is stripped and the fish disappears. Artificials must likewise be struck instantly. The latter should be fished deep. The fight of the mangrove snapper, once hooked, is furious and determined as it lashes its body in a frenzy to free itself.

Edibility
Excellent.

Weights
No established Florida record. Average: 1 - 2½ lbs., reported to 20 lbs.

Snapper, Mutton

Lutjanus analis
MUTTONFISH, MUTTON SNAPPER

Identification
The mutton snapper has yellow upper fins, bright red lower fins, a darkish spot below the back dorsal and vertical dark bars shading off to a pinkish belly.

Location
Shell and coral bottoms, reefs, off the East Coast. The southern half of the state and the Keys are the most productive. Wherever good grouper fishing is to be had, the mutton snapper is likely to be on hand. It should be considered a fairly deep-water fish for the most part, although on the Keys they move in close to shore.

Methods of Fishing, Habits
Best methods are still fishing with cut bait; slow deep troll.

The mutton snapper is a bottom-feeder and cut mullet is a top attraction to this fine food fish. They can be located by knowing the location of grouper holes or coral and shell formations which attract all bottom fish. It is difficult to fish exclusively for them, as they are usually in the company of grouper, grunts and other snapper.

The strike of the mutton snapper is strong, the fight, entirely beneath the surface, tougher than most of its bottom-fish neighbors. Slow-moving streamers and strip baits, drifting over known coral and shell formations, will bring the mutton snapper into action. Using a line free of sinkers is often rewarding.

Edibility
Excellent. Ranks with the best of the choice, succulent snapper family. Because many coaser fish can be used for chowder, mutton snapper should be reserved for broiling, steak and gourmet cooking.

Weights
Florida record: about 30 lbs. Average: 4 - 10 lbs.

Snapper, Red

Lutjanus aya
RED SNAPPER, PENSACOLA SNAPPER

Identification
"Red snapper" is possibly the most misapplied tag in Florida. Everything from redfish to mangrove snapper and muttonfish are hastily dubbed "red snapper."

The true red snapper has the same general body outlines of the snapper family, although it is heavier through the middle portion than the mangrove or lane snapper. It is a bright, almost uniform red all over, with no dark bars or markings on the back. It can be safely assumed that snapper taken from shorelines, sand bars or shallow waters are some variety other than red snapper, as they rarely move from deep waters.

Location
The greatest concentrations are in the Gulf over offshore banks in water up to 200 feet in depth. The Pensacola area is so rich in snapper banks the fish is referred to commercially as "Pensacola snapper." A few spots along the Atlantic Coast—off St. Augustine, Cape Canaveral—provide good red snapper catches. With the exception of small specimens during a migratory period, they are seldom taken in shore waters.

Methods of Fishing, Habits
Best methods are bottom fishing with cut bait and with hand-lines.

Because the red snapper inhabits such deep water, hand-line fishing with necessarily heavy weights is the most commonly used method. The fish is widely sought by market fishermen, who employ this method exclusively. And because of the tackle and essential manner of catch, the fish is not highly regarded as a game fish by sports anglers.

Edibility
The flesh remains firm for a long period, has a good flavor, ranks high as an excellent market fish. Baking recommended.

Weights
No established Florida record. Unofficial: 35 lbs., but 20 - 25 lbs. not unusual at Pensacola banks.

Snapper, Schoolmaster

Lutjanus apodus
SCHOOLMASTER

Identification
The schoolmaster snapper is a chalk-blue with pale yellow fins. Bars like thumbprints mark the upper back.

Location
Not a common snapper in Florida waters. Found occasionally in southerly areas and throughout the Keys. It consorts with other snappers and the bottom fish of the reefs.

Methods of Fishing, Habits

Caught incidentally while bottom fishing. The best baits for schoolmaster snapper as well as the fish's fighting abilities follow closely those of the mangrove snapper.

Edibility

Good.

Weights

Florida average: 3/4 - 1 lb. Reported to 5 lbs.

Snapper, Yellowtail

Ocuyurus chrysurus

YELLOWTAIL

Identification

The yellowtail is the most handsome of the snapper family. A yellow bar starts at the nose, runs through the eye to the tail. Large yellow dots mark a blue background above the lateral bar. On the lower sides and belly, narrow vertical yellow stripes stream back from the pectoral fin to the tail. The fins and the exceptionally widely forked tail are a deep golden yellow. They are more slender than other snappers.

Location

The yellowtail snapper is most numerous on the lower Keys and from Key West south and west, although taken occasionally on the lower mainland coasts. It is found over reefs, consorting chiefly with its own kind, and it schools in moderate numbers. The largest yellowtail are often solitary.

Methods of Fishing, Habits

Best method is still fishing with live shrimp, hermit crab. Will take cut bait much less avidly.

Yellowtail have the general smartness of the snapper family, and chumming with crushed crab and broken shrimp over reef waters is a splendid way to start them feeding and striking. Their strike and fight are stronger, for the most part, than those of other snappers.

Edibility

Ranked a delicacy. Yellowtail brings top market prices; the flesh is fine, white and tasty. Floridians don't rate them above the mutton or mangrove snappers, but northern markets do.

Weights

Average: 1 lb. Reported to 5 lbs.

Snook

Centropomus undecimalis

SNOOK

Identification

Anglers used to taking snook in upper Gulf states and Mexico and designating them as "robalo" will find the term "snook" used exclusively in Florida.

The snook is a long-bodied fish, with the upper part of the snout depressed and a protruding lower jaw. An immediate identifying characteristic is the pronounced dark lateral line running from the upper gill the length of the body to the center of the forked tail. Fresh-water anglers will quickly note the similarity of the shape of the body of the snook to that of the walleyed pike.

Location

Snook are confined to no one area of Florida. They cluster in quantity beneath bridges, docks, boathouses and along river banks. They move up streams and rivers to brackish and fresh waters. They prowl drainage ditches and canals, gather around jetties, lurk in the shadows of mangrove overhang on islands. On the West Coast especially, they are found feeding along beaches.

Inlets, bays and river mouths along the East Coast from St. Augustine south are productive, as are most Gulf shore waters, with heavy concentrations in the St. Lucie country, the Ten Thousand Islands, Marco Island and in the Keys back country.

Methods of Fishing, Habits

Best methods are light-tackle casting, still fishing at night with shrimp, small bait fish, trolling.

Snook are eulogized by a great following of Florida anglers as one of the most exciting of all salt-water fish to be taken on light tackle. On hooking into snook, plug casters, users of nylon jig baits on spinning tackle, salt-water fly-rods and service-reel-equipped casting rods, find themselves in for an explosive and bewildering exhibition of fury, aerial acrobatics, smartness and power that too often leaves only diminishing whorls scrawling the water's surface and the memory of a twisting, thrashing fish romping off to freedom.

Snook are wary and completely unpredictable in their feeding routine. A bank of snook lying in the shadow of a bridge or boat dock which may ignore all bait offered them today may avidly strike plugs or shrimp tomorrow, take only small live mullet the following day. In open water, on flats in the Keys back country, beneath mangrove overhang, or on beaches such as that of Marco Island, streamer flies and plugs worked on or below the surface can be productive. The same lures offered snook banked beneath a bridge might pass untouched. Generally, snook in more open waters may be successfully fished with plugs, streamers, nylon jigs (allowed to rest on the bottom and retrieved with a sharp, jerking motion), snook grouping beneath bridges and docks, demanding natural baits.

Snook feed more freely at night; an hour after dusk is worth two in the sunlight. If the night is moonlit, surface plugs will bring snook charging in for the kill. Live shrimp and small live bait-fish are a surer, less exciting method.

Roiled, murky waters along Atlantic and Gulf shore lines will many times find snook moving inshore for feed.

Their fight is a surface fight, with the snook going into the air for two, three or four successive jumps immediately on being hooked, then taking off on short, scorching runs. Their strike at a plug is such that a miss will often send the plug rocketing into the air. Practiced fly fishermen assert their smash at a streamer is as fast as that of a mountain trout, with a lot more steam behind it.

For years Florida sportsmen tried to get laws passed declaring snook a game fish, with bag limits and other protective restrictions. The well-known fishing columnist Allan Corson was a leader in this effort to preserve this truly great light-tackle game fish. It is now a gamefish by Florida law, catch limited to 4 a day.

Edibility

Excellent. Skin and filet.

Weights

World record: 50½ lbs, Florida average: 5 - 6 lbs. To 35 lbs.

At night you can often see a string of fish like this, caught with a heavy cane pole and stout line, using a wooden lure on the surface, whipping it about in the pattern of a figure "8". These are Snook ranging up to 20 pounds, all taken in the space of two hours. Bridge and pier fishing in Florida is often so fabulous it is hard to believe.

They say you might catch almost anything on the fishing boats out of Key West, and the above photograph of a Broadbill Swordfish is evidence of that truth. This rare fish is sought after with the most complicated and expensive tackle, but is seldom taken in Florida waters.

Swordfish (Broadbill)

Xiphias gladus

SWORDFISH, BROADBILL

Identification

The broadbill or swordfish is so rarely taken in Florida waters that it barely rates inclusion here.

Location

It is one of the great billed fish believed to prowl and feed deep in the Gulf Stream off the Florida coast. It is so seldom seen or hooked that year after year no record of any catch appears in the annual East Coast tournaments.

Methods of Fishing, Habits

It is a bottom-feeder at great depths, occasionally coming to the surface, seemingly in search of sunlight. Its natural cruising and feeding depths are so great that a deep troll is impossible and it should be fished with a surface troll when sighted.

Its mouth is soft and its fight a wild plunging in and out of the water. Broadbills take any interference with their free-swimming liberty as a serious personal afront, and have no hesitancy in attacking a boat.

Weights

A 103-pounder was entered in the Miami Tournament in 1952. Scattered reports of sightings occur during the winter months. They are widely fished in far northern Atlantic waters, commercial fishermen getting high prices for the firm, excellently flavored fish. World record on rod and reel: 1,182 lbs.

Tarpon

Tarpon Atlanticus

TARPON, SILVER KING

Identification

The tarpon is a heavy-bodied fish with a protruding, aggressive - looking lower jaw, mouth large and exceptionally bony. A filament streams from the back of the dorsal, often referred to as the tarpon's "feather," the back is blue to greenish-black. The scales are large, with the lower portion of each thickly coated in bright silver and the upper portion semitransparent.

Location

Tarpon are found in all Florida waters and are residents to some degree in lower areas, with huge migrations moving up both coasts, beginning in late February and continuing through July. They are a shoreline-, flats-, bay-, and inlet-fish, move into canals and rivers to brackish and fresh waters.

Although most areas of Florida can claim splendid tarpon fishing during migrations, records indicate the heaviest concentrations appear in the Gulf from the Caloosahatchee River to Clearwater in the spring and early summer months.

Methods of Fishing, Habits

Best methods are still fishing with live mullet, pinfish, shrimp, pilchards, crab; plug-casting with natural motion plugs; trolling; fly-fishing and spin-casting for smaller specimens with streamers.

Tarpon can be called everyman's game fish. It is the mightiest of the coastal fishes and to many saltwater anglers the most exciting fish

Tarpon, the Silver King of fishes on the Florida West Coast, are caught in such quantities throughout the Summer months that if it were not for the pressure of conservationists to release unharmed fish, the species might well be decimated. Three large tournaments in the Tampa Bay area offer a combined $50,000 in prizes for the capture of Tarpon. Most of these prizes are paid for released fish. This fishing party above each took one fish for a trophy.

that can be taken on medium to light tackle, magnificent in its power and explosive display of dramatic combat. It can be fished from shoreline and bridge, taken from small skiffs in protected waters, along canals and bayous and is within the reach of every fisherman with know-how who has a good rod, a few lures or a few cents' worth of bait.

On the prowl, the slug-jaw of the tarpon juts with a symbolic aggressiveness that portends the wild turbulence of water and fish once it is pricked with a hook. The great slab-sided fighter immediately takes to the air, its huge gills distended and rattling, smashing off across the surface in leap after leap, giving the appearance of a series of camera-stills pasted in the air.

No fish is more adept than the tarpon at throwing a hook. Part of this ability can be credited to the hard, bony mouth, but even more accorded to a curiously confident course of violent action pursued by the fish immediately on sensing danger. It seems almost like a practiced routine; skillful, paced, diversified.

Tarpon cruise slowly and deliberately. They prowl over flats, under mangrove, along canals, jetties, under bridges. They move from flats where they have been feeding at high water as the tide lowers, and productice fishing can be expected at such an hour in channels through which they pass.

When fishing with natural baits, a moment or two should be allowed so that the hook can be set in the hard mouth, but allowing too much time may result in gut-hooking, lessening the fight of the fish and making release futile. Tarpon will pick up dead mullet when fished on the bottom, preferably gashed or cut in big strips for greater scent attraction. They will take live shrimp drifted to them in channels. On flats and in canals, jointed plugs and streamer flies produce fine action. Floated small live mullet in deeper waters are considered sure tarpon-killers, as are live pinfish.

Tarpon feed more avidly at night than during the daylight, the hours at dusk and afterward being more rewarding to the angler both in the number of strikes and the magnificent sight of a blaze of silver surging upward into the moonlight.

Fishermen familiar with tarpon consider that a good average is one tarpon boated for every four or five hooked. A newcomer to the spectacular sport, with its wide variation of techniques, many of which are based on the particular locale, and the amazing ingenuity of the fish itself, can save time and heartbreak by employing a guide to introduce him to the ways of this magnificent game fish.

Edibility

Inedible. Always released if not desired for mounting or citation.

Weights

World record: 283 lbs. Florida to 210 lbs.

Tripletail

Lobotes surinamensis

BUOYFISH, CHOBIE

Identification

Large anal and second dorsal fins create the illusion of three tails, accounting for the name "triple." The fish is chunky, high-backed, heavy for its length. It is an over-all dark brown to black in color.

Location

The tripletail is primarily a deep-water fish, occasionally venturing shoreward to feed around docks and jetties. It has a strong liking for wrecks, buoys and underwater debris. It is not a common fish in Florida waters. Fair numbers are taken, however, in warmer months in the Cape Canaveral area on the East Coast and along the middle Gulf Coast.

Methods of Fishing, Habits

Best method is still fishing on bottom.

One of the prizes of the dock or seawall fisherman, a Tripletail offers a real tug-of-war and a wonderful dinner if captured. They live mostly in deep water, around offshore buoys. Sunken wrecks are their preferred homes. This catch shown above, was an 18-pound dish of happiness, caught off a bridge on Florida's West Coast.

Tripletail prefer shrimp, clams, will take small mullet, whitebait, squid. Artificial lures are a poor gamble.

Tripletail should be fished directly at buoys, close to jetties, alongside a sunken wreck. Their strike is fast and hard. The runs, although short, are especially strong and rough-and-tumble. When hooked, they throw their body into a curve that allows the use of their broad sides and wide fins to increase their resistance. They do not jump.

Edibility

Excellent. The flesh is white and fine-textured.

Weights

Florida average: 6 - 8 lbs. To 30 lbs.

Tuna, Atlantic Blackfin

Thunnus atlanticus

ALBACORE, BLACKFIN TUNA

Identification

The term "albacore" will probably long persist with Florida anglers, although "blackfin tuna" is often used. The full name now accredited in authoritative check lists of "Atlantic blackfin tuna" is not employed by Florida fishermen and guides.

The blackfin tuna is a gleaming deep blue on the back, vivid yellow at the pectoral line, silvery on the belly. The pectoral fin is exceptionally long, allowing the angler an easy point of identification. Fins are black.

Location

The albacore schools with bonitos and other tunas, and is a deepwater fish, found almost exclusively in the Gulf Stream. In Florida it is infrequently found north of the Keys and is taken chiefly from February through June. At no point is it a common fish.

Methods of Fishing, Habits

Best method is trolling, usually deep. Baits the same as for bonitos and little tuna.

The albacore is another of the bonito-tuna-shaped fish which hit with a terrible thud, going into a quivering, powerful tugging that strains medium-light tackle. Inasmuch as they travel in small schools, once one is hooked and boated the area should be circled for companions.

Edibility

Good. Should be boiled, broiled and baked. Meat whitens with cooking.

Weights

World record: 20 lbs., 12 oz. Florida average: 8 lbs. to 20 lbs.

Tuna, Atlantic Yellowfin

Thunnus albacares

ALLISON TUNA

Identification

The back of the Allison tuna is a deep blue. The dorsal and anal fins, which form long streamers reaching to the tail, are a brilliant canary yellow. The silver sides shade to a golden yellow breast and a silver white belly.

There is constant controversy about this fish, many experts considering the yellowfin and Allison to be the same tuna, the variations resulting from growth or sex stages. The Florida angler should settle for the name "Allison tuna," the name exclusively applied in Florida waters.

Location

In Florida the range of the Allison tuna is considered the Keys area and the southern East Coast. It is an uncommon-to-scarce fish, is always found in deep water, on outside reefs, at the edge of the Gulf Stream or in it.

Methods of Fishing, Habits

Best method is trolling with heavy gear. The Allison tuna can be classified as an incidental catch, taken while trolling outer reefs or the Gulf Stream for other fish. It strikes the usual Stream-trolled baits, metal-headed feathers, strip baits and whole mullet. The strike is indescribably savage, ranking with or outdoing the explosive smash of the much heavier mighty bluefin tuna, and endurance in the sleek, stream-lined body seems endless. The angler who lands one can consider he has made a prize catch.

Edibility

Good. Brine-soak a half-hour before cooking.

Weights

World record: 265 lbs. Florida average: 60 - 100 lbs.

Tuna, Bluefin

Thunnus Thynnus

BLUEFIN TUNA

Reached solely by expensive charter to the Bahamas from south Florida fishing centers. The mighty bluefin appears only on the eastern edge of the Stream in late April and May, during its spawning and northward migration periods. Cat Cay and Bimini areas are most widely favored.

Highly skilled crews, special heavy gear, well-muscled and "well-heeled" fishermen are prerequisites.

Tuna, Little

Euthynnus alletteratus

FALSE ALBACORE, LITTLE TUNA

Identification

The term "little tuna" is rapidly becoming accepted in many quarters, but anglers in Florida will find the name "false albacore" still widely used.

The little tuna has a deep blue back, with irregular serrated markings above the lateral line from the middle of the fish to the tail. Five or six black dots mark the silvery belly below the pectoral fin.

Location

The little tuna, primarily a deep-water fish, swims in the company of the bonitos or in the same waters. It is found on both Florida coasts and in the Straits of Florida, schooling more densely during the late spring and summer months.

Methods of Fishing, Habits

Best method is trolling well below surface with strip baits or tin squid.

The little tuna follows the feeding and striking habits of the bonitos, not responding to surface trolling as readily. Their fight is a hard, jerky tugging at the line, following a jolting strike.

Edibility

Fair, if brined for an hour or more before cooking.

Weights

Florida average: 3 - 5 lbs.

Wahoo

Acabthocybium solandri

WAHOO

Identification

The body patterns of the wahoo conform to those of the smaller mackerels with an overall appearance of being more tubular in shape. A slate-blue back shades to silvery sides with distinct vertical markings, closely spaced, visible while the fish is alive, especially sharply defined in smaller specimens. These markings blur and disappear as the fish dies. The front dorsal is of exceptional length and regular in outline. The tail, although wide-winged, is more squared off than the deeply forked tails of the other mackerel. The teeth are jagged and large.

Location

Wahoo are found in the Gulf Stream and adjacent waters over the outer reefs. They range well out in deep waters of the Gulf. On Florida's East Coast, the greatest frequency of wahoo occurs from Palm Beach south. In no area is it numerous or common.

Methods of Fishing, Habits

Best method is trolling, with strip bait, whole mullet, feathers.

The startling and thrilling strike of the incredibly fast wahoo is often prefaced by a flash of color as much as 50 feet from the lure when the wahoo goes into his surging race for the kill.

Thus its strike is one of the most electrifying of all game fish. A confusing and often dangerous immediate course of action by the wahoo is to make an unbroken run after striking directly toward the boat and angler, giving the impression the fish has missed and the line is free. This first run is voted by many anglers the fastest ever experienced, and certainly qualifies as one of the wildest bids for freedom made by any game fish. The fight that follows—lightning changes of pace and direction occurring without warning—is an all-out bruising conflict, and wahoo, when subdued, are often very near death.

The wahoo is a comparatively scarce fish, never schools in Florida waters and is considered a prize catch by any angler fortunate enough to bring one to gaff.

Edibility

Splendid. Should be steaked in kingfish fashion. This scarce fish should always be released if not desired for food or mounting.

Weights

World-Florida record: 136 lbs. Florida average: 20 - 30 lbs., up to 65 lbs.

Whiting, Silver

Menticirrhus littoralis

GULF KING WHITING, WHITING

Identification

A silvery-sided fish, white-bellied, tarnished silver back. A fairly slender fish with a comparatively small mouth.

Location

Most frequent along upper Gulf Coast, in the low surf on sandy beaches or in bays having sandy bottoms.

Methods of Fishing, Habits

Caught while bottom-fishing the surf with shrimp or crab. The strike is nibbling and light. Just vaguely gets over the line as a game fish.

Edibility

Fair as a pan fish.

Average: ½ - ¾ lb. Have been reported to 2½ lbs.

Whiting, Southern

Menticirrhus americanus

KING WHITING, WHITING

Slanted wide dark lattice-like bars mark the silvery sides. The belly is a whitish-silver. Found along the Atlantic Coast over sandy bottoms in bays and surf. It is exclusively a bottom-feeder. In edibility, fighting qualities, and weight it compares to the Gulf king whiting.

Unusual Salt-Water Fish

Scarce, Colorful and Unusual Salt-Water Fish

With perhaps a few objections as to classification and omission, the following fish are noted because they are occasionally caught or observed while the Florida angler is pursuing the more commonly sought game fish. They are included as an aid to the sports fishermen in identifying some colorful or curiously-shaped stranger that appears on the end of a line or swims indifferently by during a day's fishing. Some are bait fish. A few are fish which are caught fairly frequently, but are not generally included in checklists of the principal salt-water game fishes.

Angelfish

ANGELFISH, COMMON
Angelichthys isabelita

ANGELFISH, BLACK
Pomocanthus arcuatus

ANGELFISH, FRENCH
Pomocanthus paru

ANGELFISH, QUEEN
Angelichthys cilaris

ROCK BEAUTY
Holocanthus tricolor

The principal habitation of the angelfish in Florida, except for the common angelfish, is the southern tip and the Keys. As for the black angelfish and rock beauty, the Key West area can be considered the only location where they are found with any frequency. The common angelfish is found as far north as Fernandina Beach.

Angelfish are all painted beauties that flash handsomely in the translucent waters of the Keys. The queen and common angelfish and the rock beauty have a curious, squared-off paddle shape and are high-profiled, with the pouting small mouth common to all angelfish.

The black angelfish has a grayish body, with every scale dotted with black, giving it a thick polkadot appearance. The French angelfish is black, with each scale tipped with yellow and the bases of the pectoral fin and tail banded in yellow. Both have wide dorsal and pectoral fins.

Common and queen angelfish are similar in coloration, with bright blue tippings and markings on fin rims. The mouth and pectoral fin contrast with the deep yellow of the body and tail fin.

The queen angelfish is the largest of the family, exceeding 20 inches in length. A circular eyelike spot on the head differentiates the queen from the common angelfish.

The rock beauty is a sharp contrast of solid black from pectoral fin to tail, with an encircling ribbon of yellow, a black-lipped mouth, blue-smudged eyes, yellow head and breast.

Angelfish, darting around rocks, pilings, bridges and over reefs, will nip at small bits of shrimp and can be taken on a tiny hook. They have little or no value as food and their capture is solely for satisfying one's curiosity about their magnificent coloration or for mounting purposes.

Balao

Hyporhamphus roberti

BALLYHOO

The balao is a widely used bait fish in Florida and is a special favorite with outer reef and Gulf Stream anglers.

It averages five inches in length, goes to 10 or 12 inches. It is a long, slender fish with a blue back, silvery sides and belly. It is easily recognized and differentiated from the similarly-shaped needlefish by the dwarfed upper beak. The balao is sometimes referred to as the "half-beak."

Batfish, Short-Nosed

Waders of Keys flats and bonefishermen occasionally stray across this curious, little fish squatting on its haunches on a grass bed. Coal black, infrequently dotted in white, it spreads its wing fins to sit with belligerently raised head. The head is small, beaked and ferocious-looking. It is as wide as it is long when in prone position, with the tail narrow and small. It will ignore baits, even those placed directly at its mouth, eying the waders in a threatening fashion, and should be avoided, as the tiny jaws are capable of a painful nip.

Blue Tang

Acanthurus coerulus

The blue tang is found chiefly in the Keys area, adding a vivid splash of color over inner reefs and around bridge pilings. When waters are warm, blue tang are occasionally taken in the southern section of mainland waters.

The tang shows a deep vivid blue over the entire body. During certain color phases it has pale yellow serrated markings flowing laterally from the head. The mouth is sharply "lipsticked" in a grayish-white. Two body spikes at the base of the tail are erected when the fish is fighting—resisting other fish or seeking its freedom from a hook. It will take some crustaceans. Mounting value only.

Unusual Salt-Water Fish

Boxfish, Spiny

Chilomycterus schoepfii

One of the "puffers," with brown serrated markings over a yellowish body. It inflates on being attacked or hooked. Spikes, or spines, protrude sharply from the back and sides. Crustacean feeder. Average seven inches in length. Curiosity value only.

Cowfish

Lactophrys tricornis

Smaller than the trunkfish, averaging eight inches, and found in most Florida waters, the cowfish is high-profiled and shows blue broken-link markings over a yellow body. Curiosity value only.

Cutlassfish

Trichiurus lepturus

A mouthful of fang-shaped teeth, a body formed like a flat-sided eel and a body-long soft dorsal that merges with the tail make this racing striker easily identifiable.

The silver-sided fish averages 2 lbs., although it goes to 6, and is caught along the middle and lower Florida East Coast. It is not prejudiced in its feeding and is liable to strike natural baits and lures while bottom-fishing, trolling or casting in bay areas. Reported by the adventurous as excellent eating.

Doctorfish

Acanthurus hepatus

High profile, tiny beaklike mouth and dark vertical score-markings over a greenish-brown body easily identify the doctorfish. Fins are often orchidaceous in color. It is found over reefs and in the waters of the Keys, is seldom hooked because of its tiny mouth. No value.

Filefish

FILEFISH, COMMON

Stephanolepis hispidus

FILEFISH, ORANGE

Ceratacanthus schoepfi

The filefishes have wedge-shaped heads, are high-bodied, with the eyes set well up on the forehead. Both have single spine dorsals.

The common filefish varies from green-grey to light gray in older specimens. The orange filefish is usually a brown-tinted orange.

Both are found in all Florida waters, but are far from common. They are sometimes taken in bottom-fishing with small crustaceans. Curiosity value only.

Hogfish, Spanish

Bodianus rufa

Occasionally taken in Keys waters. A dazzling fish, with top forward part of body a brilliant blue and the balance, a bright yellow. The scales have a peculiar metallic appearance, being heavy and ovally oblong in shape. Member of the wrasse family. Feeds with hogfish and other bottom fish. Good food value.

Houndfish

Strongylura raphidomia

A long slender fish, identical in shape with the needle-fish, except that the beak is shorter and stronger-appearing. They grow to greater size than the needlefish, and are a hazard to night fishermen in skiffs displaying lights, as they have an unpleasant habit of leaping forward in the air like a plunging rapier. They are blue-green on the back, shading off to silver on the sides and belly. They strike small strip- and feather-baits and go into a dancing fight.

Lizardfish

Synodus foetens

Very similar in shape to the snakefish and easily differentiated by its color. It has a criss cross pattern of markings in a reddish-brown to a sandy yellow, running the entire length of the upper body. Broken vertical lines in a brownish-red show over the whitish lower sides down to the underbelly. Eyes protrude above the snout. The lizardfish is usually larger than the snakefish. No value.

Lookdown

Selene vomer

A slim, high-bodied fish the set of whose eyes in a steep profile bears out its name. A flashing silvery iridescence picks up color, making the fish extremely handsome.

The lookdown is chiefly a night-feeder, is caught in average weights of ¾ to 1 lb., but goes to 3. It will hit tiny artificial lures, shrimp, bits of crab.

It is found mostly in south Florida and the Keys, usually around pilings and over shell bottoms. The flesh is fine and tasty.

Unusual Salt-Water Fish

Morays

Moray, Green

Gymnothorax funebris

The green moray, identical in shape with the spotted moray, is usually a bright grass-green in color, and is generally a larger eel than any of its relatives, often four to six feet long. The mouths of all the morays are sinister looking, a narrow slit thickly filled with vicious teeth.

Both the green and spotted morays are unwillingly caught in quantity by fishermen in the Keys—and to a lesser degree—by those on the lower Gulf Coast while bottom-fishing. Immediately on being hooked, morays start a twisting, curling motion, wrapping the line around themselves, and come aboard snapping and writhing. Although considered seriously poisonous, they are not, their danger lying in being able to inflict a sharp bite which, if the protective slime enters, will cause a bad and painful sore. They should never be handled, and unless an angler is short of tackle, best recommendation on hooking a moray is to cut the line.

Morays lie beneath rocks, in holes, waiting to pounce on small live fish. They should be watched for by waders, although no cases of a wader's being attacked can be authenticated. Their protective coloration makes them difficult to see, especially the spotted moray.

Moray, Brown — Moray, Ocellated

The brown moray—a light brown with fins tipped in black—and the ocellated moray—a darker brown, also with the dorsal showing a black rim — are less frequent, although the ocellated moray is fairly common in some Gulf areas.

Venturesome gourmets have been known to declare their flesh good. Florida locals consider them poisonous. Their repulsive appearance, difficulty in handling and questionable edibility make them a catch that should be discarded except by the experimenter.

Moray, Spotted

Gymnothorax moringa

The most common moray, or moray eel, is the spotted moray. It is almost identical in shape with the other members of the family, differentiated by its coloration. It is an over-all muddy yellow in color, heavily dotted in brown. Its hide is tough, covered with a thick slime, a long soft dorsal running from the head around the tail portion to the midsection of the belly.

Needlefish

Tylosurus raphidoma

Needlefish dart and glide along the surface of all Florida waters, their long jaws picking up bits of food and tiny fish, with whitebait a favorite. They are greenish and silvery. They are easily distinguished from the balao by the corresponding long jaws, as contrasted with the long lower jaw and upper beak of the balao. They grow to much greater lengths, have no food value.

Palometa

Trachinotus glaucus

PALOMETA, LONG-FINNED POMPANO

The palometa, the most dazzling member of the pompano family, is listed under this classification because it is rare and is taken only incidentally while fishing for pompano.

Palometa are high-backed, with the second dorsal flowing in a streamer that creates a sweeping, upward outline from the nose of the fish to the back tip of the fin.

The belly is a golden yellow, the breast, rose-flushed, the upper sides a sky-blue. Four darkish widely separated vertical lines give the appearance of the sides having been marked with a soft crayon.

They are not considered in the gourmet division accorded the pompano but are still excellent eating.

Parrotfish

These colorful fish get to be "homebodies" to Keys residents who have docks on their property. They cluster around bridge and dock pilings and patrol short distances along rocky Keys shores, seldom evidencing fear on being approached.

Parrotfish Blue

Scarus caeruleus

The blue parrotfish is especially evident in the translucent Keys waters. It is normally found in somewhat smaller sizes than the rainbow parrotfish. Although it is almost identical in shape, its white beaklike mouth and lurid blue color easily differentiate it.

Although their fight is not strong, the bony mouths of the parrotfish are amazingly strong in their bite and they can easily twist the best hook into a shapeless mass. They strike unexpectedly at live shrimp, after having ignored the bait for the preceding half-hour.

Unusual Salt-Water Fish

Parrotfish, Rainbow

Pseudoscarus guacamai

The larger rainbow parrotfish is multicolored, with shades of orange and green showing brightly on the sides, while the dorsal varies from orange to blue. The mouth is the same pursed bony beak as the blue parrotfish. These ornamental fish should never be killed unless desired for mounting. Their flesh is worthless.

Pinfish

Lagodon rhomboides

A small fish, with the body a brilliant yellow with clearly defined blue lateral stripes running the length of the fish. All the fins show yellow markings.

The pinfish makes a fine pan fish if one wants to bother with anything this small; the fish seldom goes above 8 or 9 inches. It provides an excellent bait for large game fish, as hardy qualities permit keeping it alive and active with far less trouble than in the case of small mullet and other bait fishes.

Pudding-Wife

Iridio radiatus

A member of the wrasse family, the pudding-wife is a garishly-colored fish of blues, greens, oranges and yellows with a thick overlay of bluish-green tear-shaped dots, occasionally taken on the Keys. It has a small mouth and a long, even dorsal. A noticeable, thick slime makes handling a problem. It goes to a weight of 3 pounds. Not eaten.

Rabbitfish

Lagocephalus laevigatus

The largest of the "puffer fish," the rabbitfish swells for protection when taken from the water. Its skin is smooth except for a prickly forward belly. The head is larger than other puffers, the back is a light-green and the small, bony mouth is constructed like a pair of cutting pliers. It feeds around pilings and ramps.

Although promptly rejected by many as a trash fish, the rabbitfish is almost a delicacy. The easiest method of preparation is to cut the fish just about in half, making the cut cross-body at the end of the prickly belly section and also using the remaining tail-section of the body, which should be skinned. The meat is delicious when deep-fried or pan-fried, rolled in cornmeal. The rabbitfish is found in all Florida waters.

Remora

Echeneis naucrates

The curiously-equipped remora has an oval-shaped plate on the top of its head, which is ribbed like a rubber mat. This is a suction cup which the remora uses to attach itself to larger, faster fish, sharks being especially preferred. Its suction may be safely ascertained by placing the hand firmly over the head.

The remora clamps onto the belly or side of a shark, releasing itself to feed after the shark has gorged and left torn bits of food in the water. Free-swimming, the remora will take small baits and will sometimes detach itself to strike cut bait or small live bait in its path.

A wide black stripe flows from the lips of the fish back through the tail, contrasting with the whitish-gray body. Its average length is $1\frac{1}{2}$ ft.

Sand-Diver

Synodus intermedius

The sand-diver, a member of the lizardfish family, is brown to tan with light orange markings. Caught almost exclusively over sand, it appears to dive into sand on being alarmed. Its strike is similar to that of the snakefish. No value.

Sandfish

Diplectrum formosum

SAND PERCH

A small fish, tan or sand-colored with blue broken-link stripes and vertical dark markings extending from the dorsal to upper belly. The tail is brightly dotted with red and yellow. A fine pan fish and a good little fighter on the lightest tackle. Length: 6-8 inches. Found in all Florida waters.

Sargassum

Histrio pictus

The best description of a sargassum might be that of a Conch (a native of Key West) who, on seeing one nibbling on a floating weedbed, looked at it incredulously and muttered, "It just ain't so." Spiked, multicolored, mottled, with a headdress effect of fins and frondlike decoration, the tiny sargassum (5 to 7 inches) presents an over-all apearance of a primitive chieftain in festive dress. Rare. Found in the waters of the Keys.

Unusual Salt-Water Fish

When you catch one of these, be ready to find a nice shore to beach your boat. Sawfish, which will take a bait in shallow water can cut your boat up or take off your leg, if you get too close. The fish above measured 18-feet long and was "led" ashore after being hooked off Anna Maria Island. For such well armed creatures, they are exceedingly docile on the end of a line.

Sawfish

Pristis pectinatus

Sawfish are occasionally seen, less occasionally hooked in Florida waters, especially along the Gulf Coast and in the Keys.

The fish is a member of the shark family. It is an over-all brown color, with a wide, flat bill from which large, sharp teeth protrude, saw-fashion. The fish uses its bill as a maiming, killing weapon, making it extremely dangerous to handle. Florida commercial fishermen have been seriously injured trying to remove a thrashing sawfish from their nets.

Sawfish will strike live baits. They are declared to be very palatable by those who have eaten them. Anglers landing one of these not-too-common fish often cut off the bill, or saw, for a memento.

Scorpionfish

Scorpaena plumeri

Rather ridiculous-looking, it vies with the sargassum as a multicolored object, with the fins giving the appearance of having been "pinked" by a tailor. Its dominant colors include reds, blues and greens. The tail is banded and mottled with browns and yellows.

The scorpionfish should never be touched. The front dorsal carries tiny loads of poison which will make painful sores if the sharp spines come in contact with the hand. Curiosity value only.

Sergeant-Major

Abudefduf saxatilis

A litle oval-shaped fellow found fairly frequently in Keys areas darting over rocks and around bridge pilings. It is usually no longer than 3 or 4 inches, showing broad vertical dark bands over a muddy yellow.

Decorative value only.

Unusual Salt-Water Fish

Snakefish

Trachinocephalus myops

One of the lizardfish family, the snakefish has a large, flat reptile-appearing head and a triangular-shaped mouth with fine pin-sharp teeth. It runs from 5 to 9 inches in length and will strike a trolled lure larger than itself, making a lightning strike and fighting furiously. It usually appears over sand or mud flats. No value.

Spadefish

Chaetodipterus faber

The spadefish is oval-shaped, with a white body and wide vertical black bands that continue in flowing lines through the large trailing second dorsal and anal fins. The mouth is small. The sharply-contrasting black bands fade noticeably as the fish ages.

Unlike many of the more dazzlingly-marked fish of subtropic waters, the spadefish grows to respectable size, having been reported up to 12 pounds. It groups in considerable numbers over reefs and wrecks, feeds on crustaceans and is a fast striker. A fair table fish.

Squirrelfish

Holocentrus ascensionis

The squirrelfish is a brilliant red in color, shading to a whitish-pink belly. The dorsals are yellow, red-tipped. The large protruding eyes, dark, liquid and personable, make its identification easy.

Mostly night-feeders, they are caught on the Keys, the only area where they appear with any regularity, while anglers are bottom-fishing with shrimp or crab.

Not too desirable as a table fish.

Toadfish

Opsanus tau

A scavenger annoyance to bottom-fishermen, the toadfish latches onto almost any bait and, in areas such as the Indian River, seems to carpet the bottom. The jaw is built like a pair of wire pliers and the fish's disposition is such that it should not be handled without the use of fishermen's pliers.

Slimy, and anything but appetizing in appearance, early Florida anglers have nevertheless learned that, by chopping the large head off well back on the body and then skinning the remainder of the body in a simple "peeling" operation, the cone-shaped chunk of tail meat provides quite a delicacy.

Triggerfish

TRIGGERFISH, COMMON

Balistes carolinensis

TRIGGERFISH, OCEAN

Canthidermis sabaco

TRIGGERFISH, QUEEN

Balistes vetula

The triggerfishes persistently nip portions of crustacean baits from anglers fishing around pilings and Keys reefs as long as they are offered, without permitting themselves to be hooked. This is due to their darting, suspicious strike and their extremely small mouths.

All three are high-profiled, high-bodied. The common triggerfish is somewhat more rounded in head outline, is an off-brown with yellowish high back dorsal.

The ocean triggerfish, as its name implies, inhabits deeper waters and is caught over the outer reefs. A yellow piping marks the mouth and the pectoral fin. The over-all color is a slate-blue. On the Keys, local fishermen dub them "ocean tally."

The queen triggerfish is a luridly colored affair, almost artificial-looking in its regularity of markings. A blue marked mouth contrasts with an orange breast; the back is green with veinlike wavy lines around the eyes, creating a sunburst effect. The dorsal and anal fins are a startling blue, with a long filament trailing off the second dorsal.

Weights

Weights of triggerfishes run from a top for the common triggerfish of about 4 pounds to 6 pounds for the queen triggerfish and the ocean triggerfish.

Trumpetfish

Aulostomus maculatus

Aptly named, from the standpoint of its elongated, snouted body, this small-mouthed curiosity is not for hook-and-line fishermen. The tail is spade-shaped and dark dots mark the length of its yellow-bluish body. It ranges in size from 10 to 20 inches. It is usually observed chasing tiny fish.

Trunkfish

Lactophrys trigonus

A humpbacked gray fish, with a black saddlemark and a black-tipped tail, not going above 10 inches in length. It rates as a delicacy in Key West. It has the appearance of being "packed for shipping," encased in a shell-like bony structure. The mouth is a beak. It is often called "boxfish" on the Keys.

Salt-Water Fishing Areas

The salt-water fishing areas of Florida have been divided here into nine sections, beginning at the uppermost point of Florida's East Coast, continuing down the Atlantic to the Keys, across Florida Bay and up the Gulf Coast to the far western tip of the state at Gulf Beach.

No attempt has been made to be exhaustive in enumerating the fish an angler may take at any particular town or section. Of the vast number of Florida salt-water fish, overlappings of ranges and duplications make it impossible to list all the fish that may be caught at any given point. It is difficult to be exact, in many cases, about the greatest frequency of fish in a particular area. The great sweeping migrations of some game fish, the sometimes baffling concentrations of species in areas not ordinarily frequented, the cycles of numerousness—all these make it necessary to highlight the species known to be prevalent in the various areas, to offer the average angler a working knowledge of what he may expect to catch in any general area.

It is possible to be specific, of course, with some outstanding game fish. For all practical angling purposes, bonefish can be considered as principally inhabiting the lower tip of the East Coast (Section 3), and the Keys. From the records available, sailfish, although caught the length of Florida's Atlantic Coast are found most frequently in the Stuart-Palm Beach area. On the other hand, tarpon range all Florida waters during their migrations, and although their greatest frequencies are listed both under areas and under the specific fish, with Section Seven (Boca Grande, Useppa, etc.) noted as especially famed, resident anglers in many towns throughout the state will offer their particular locale as a magnificent tarpon spot. A snook fisherman at Everglades City or around Marco may cast a jaundiced eye at any claim made by residents of the St. Lucie country (Section Three) regarding its splendid snook fishing. And, of course, the seatrout fishermen of the Indian River country sometimes find it hard to believe tales of fine trout-fishing in the Keys back country or off Gulf Coast beaches.

The tabulations below may seem to resolve themselves into generalities, but they are generalities which have been carefully worked out to provide a practical guide for the visiting angler.

Rarest of the rare this Luvaris Imperialis, which looks something like a Tuna, was captured in the Gulf of Mexico by Jim Kelley, a veteran fisherman. The fish weighed in at 180 pounds and when docked was soon cut up for steaks. The flavor was delicious. Only 37 of these fish have ever been reported in the world.

Towns, cities and fishing centers listed in each section are followed by notations of the outstanding fish and catches made in that area, together with the regular catches a fisherman may expect. The top seasons for some of the principal fish are also recorded. For further detail about the frequency of a particular fish in any area, the season and type of water in which it is found, the reader should refer to the specific fish under Salt-Water Sport Fishes.

Salt-Water Fishing Areas

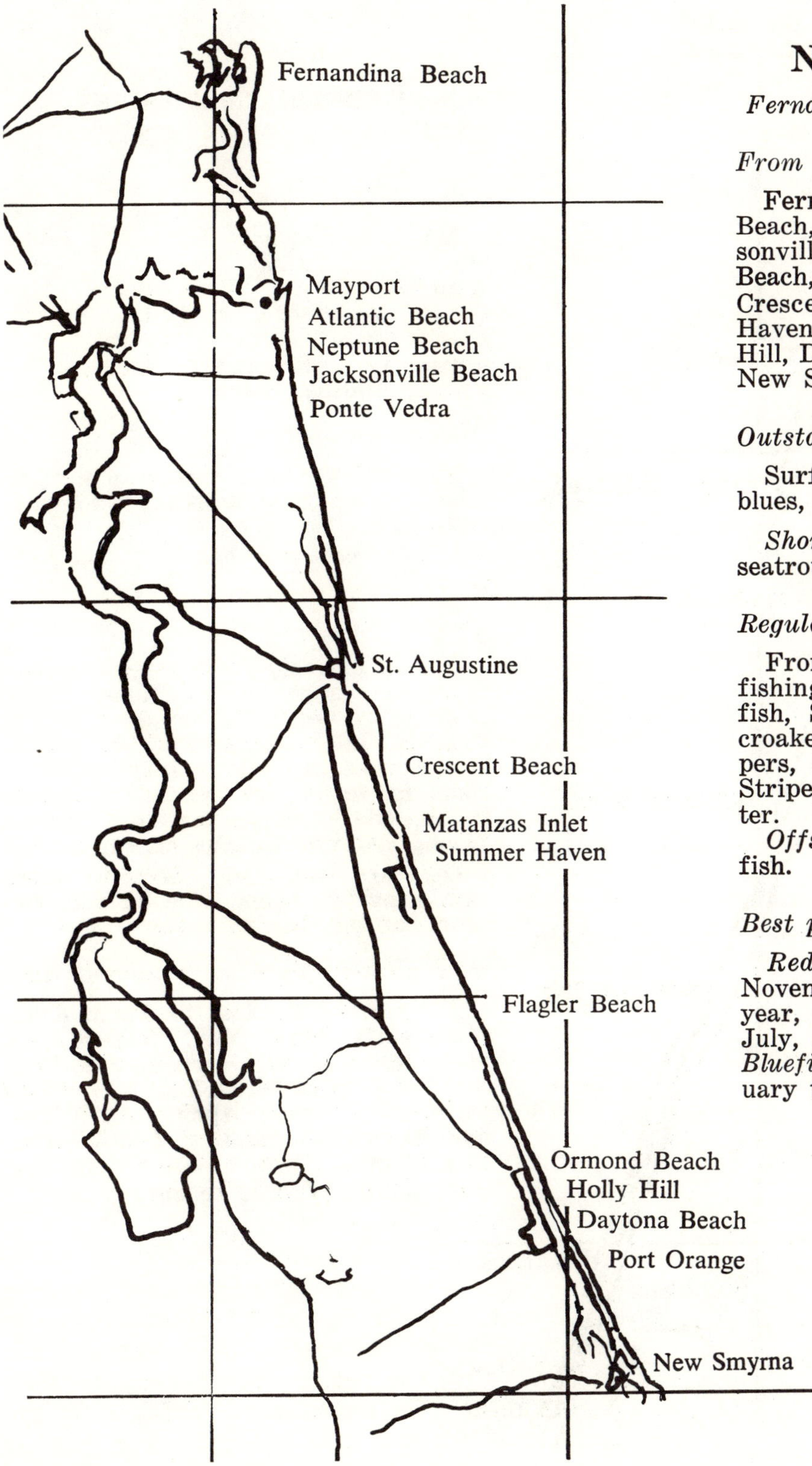

Section One

Northeast Atlantic Coast

Fernandina Beach to New Smyrna Beach

From north to south

Fernandina Beach, Mayport, Atlantic Beach, Neptune Beach, Jacksonville, Jacksonville Beach, Ponte Vedra, Ponte Vedra Beach, St. Augustine, St. Augustine Beach, Crescent Beach, Matanzas Inlet, Summer Haven, Flagler Beach, Ormond Beach, Holly Hill, Daytona, Daytona Beach, Port Orange, New Smyrna Beach.

Outstanding

Surf-casting for redfish (channel bass), blues, drum.

Shoreline: inlets, rivers, bays—speckled seatrout, redfish, drum, sheepshead, blues.

Regular Catches

From beaches, bridges, ocean piers, skiff fishing in bays, rivers, inlets: redfish, bluefish, Spanish mackerel, speckled seatrout, croakers, flounders, snook, ladyfish, snappers, bottom fish. Tarpon (summer). Striped bass (St. Johns River) early winter.

Offshore and Gulf Stream: sailfish, kingfish.

Best periods for some principal fish

Redfish—all year, greatest frequencies November through April. *Seatrout* — all year, late spring outstanding. *Tarpon* — July, early August. *Kingfish*—April, May. *Bluefish*—November to May. *Sailfish*—January to April. *Drum*—all year.

Salt-Water Fishing Areas

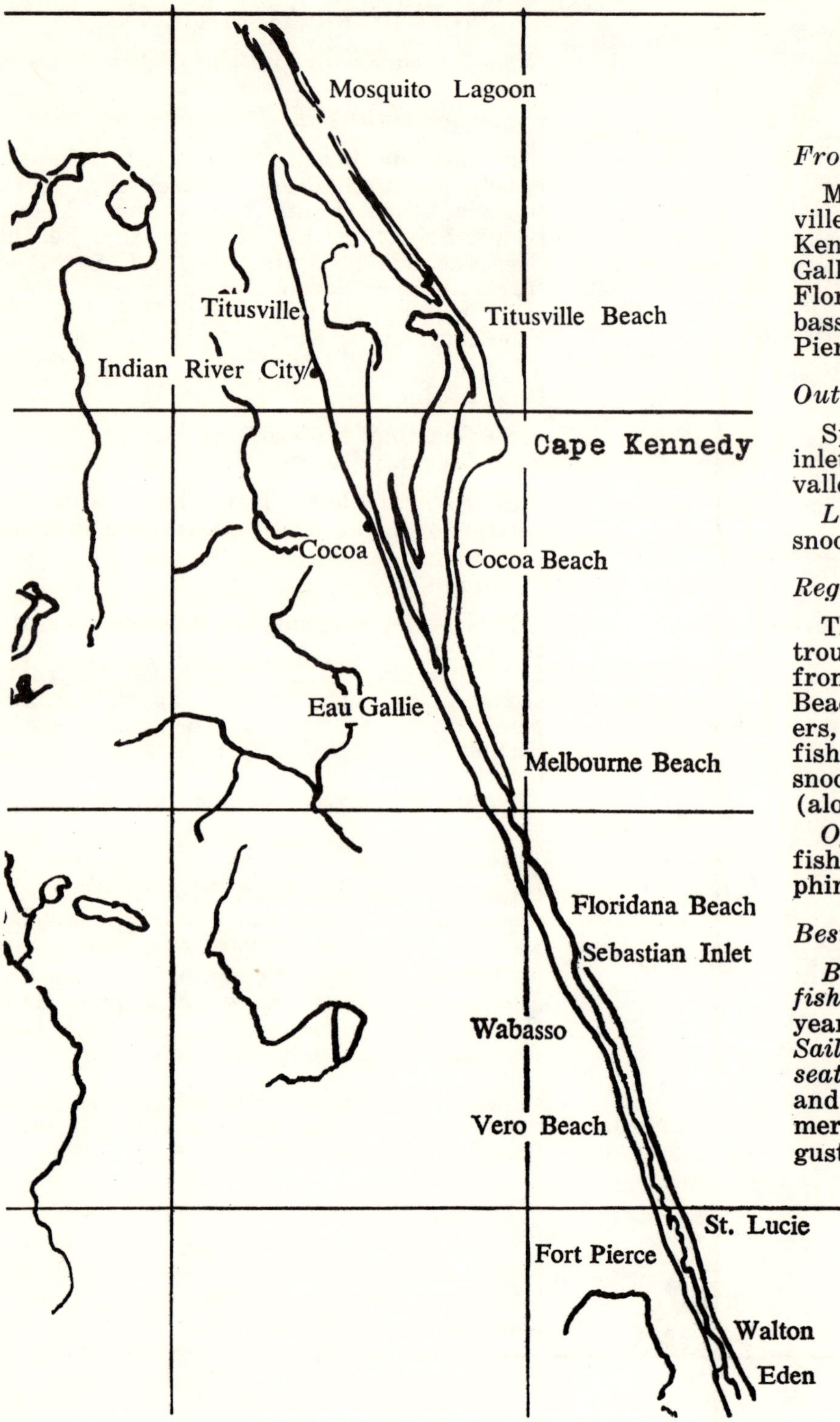

Section Two

Central East Coast

Indian River Country

From north to south

Mosquito Lagoon, Titusville, Titusville Beach, Indian River City, Cape Kennedy, Cocoa, Cocoa Beach, Eau Gallie, Melbourne, Melbourne Beach, Floridana Beach, Sebastian Inlet, Wabasso, Vero Beach, St. Lucie, Fort Pierce, Walton, Eden.

Outstanding

Speckled seatrout, redfish in surf, in inlets—drum, tripletail (chobie), crevalle jack.

Lower portions of area: sailfish, snook.

Regular Catches

The extensively fished speckled seatrout the length of the Indian River from shore, seawall, bridge, skiffs Beaches, inlets, bays—redfish, croakers, crevalle jack, drum, ladyfish, bluefish, mackerel, sheepshead, snapper, snook, tripletail, pompano, tarpon (along Atlantic beaches in summer).

Offshore and Gulf Stream: Reef fish, kingfish, cobia, blue runner, dolphin, sailfish, bonito, tunas.

Best periods for some principal fish

Bluefish — October to April. *Kingfish*—early April, May. *Redfish* — all year, October to April outstanding. *Sailfish*—December to March. *Speckled seatrout*—all year, April to early July and August outstanding. *Snook*—summer months. *Tarpon*—June, July, August, along Atlantic beaches.

Salt-Water Fishing Areas

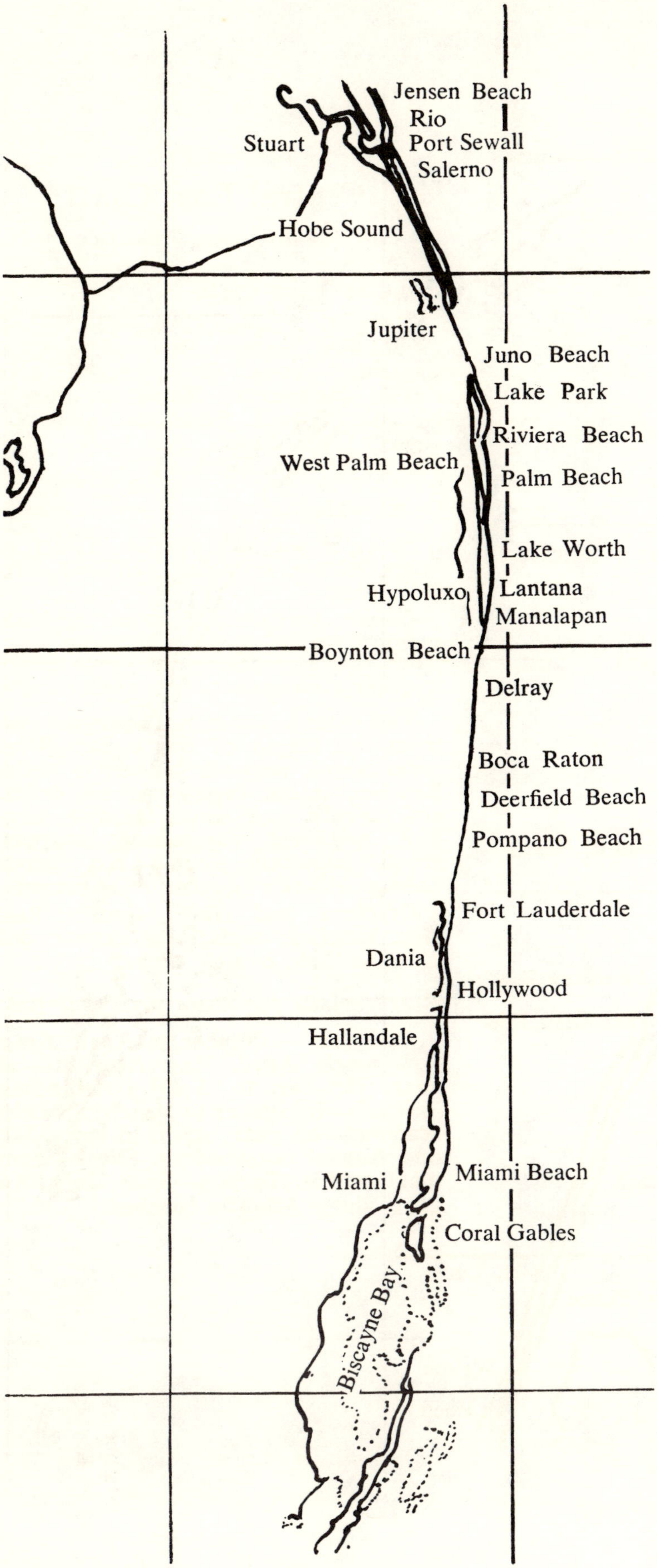

Section Three

Lower East Coast

Jensen Beach to Lower Biscayne Bay

From north to south

Jensen Beach, Rio, Stuart, Port Sewall, Salerno, Hobe Sound, Jupiter, Juno Beach, Lake Park, Riviera Beach, West Palm Beach, Palm Beach, Lake Worth, Lantana, Hypoluxo, Manalapan, Boynton Beach, Delray, Boca Raton, Deerfield Beach, Pompano Beach, Fort Lauderdale, Dania, Hollywood, Hallandale, Miami Beach, Miami, Coral Gables, Biscayne Bay.

Outstanding

Sailfishing in entire area—Stuart to the Palm Beaches especially noted.

Gulf Stream: sail, white marlin, Allison tuna, mako, blue marlin, dolphin.

Shoreline: snook, tarpon, seatrout, redfish, snapper—blues and mackerel during migrations.
Lower portion of area: bonefish.

Regular Catches

From beaches, bridges, ocean piers, skiff-fishing in bays, inlets, rivers: bluefish, redfish, gaff-topsail, Spanish mackerel, speckled seatrout, croakers, flounder, ladyfish, grunts, pompano, crevalle jack, blue runner, snappers, sheepshead, snook.

Offshore and Gulf Stream: sailfish, white marlin, blue marlin, wahoo, bonitos, tuna, dolphin, mako shark.

Reef and offshore: barracuda, red grouper, Warsaw grouper, cobia, kingfish, mackerel, amberjack, snappers.

Best periods for some principal fish

Bluefish — early October to December. Fair all winter. *Bonefish*—late spring, summer. *Dolphin*—late spring, early summer. *Kingfish*—November, midspring. *Reef fish* —all year. *Sailfish*—December to March. *Seatrout* — March to July. *Tarpon* — late April to mid-August. *White marlin*—March, early April.

Salt-Water Fishing Areas

Section Four

The Keys

Key Largo to Key West, Overseas Highway, The Marquesas, Dry Tortugas

From north to south

Jewfish Creek, Key Largo, Tavernier, Islamorada, Lower Matecumbe, Craig, Long Key, Marathon, Bahia Honda, Big Pine Key, Key West.

Outstanding

Upper portion: seatrout, redfish, snappers. Key Largo, Upper and Lower Matecumbe, Long Key, Marathon—finest Florida flats for bonefish. Permit, tarpon on medium light tackle. Fishing for entire range of reef fish the length of the Keys, with especially heavy concentrations of barracuda, grouper and amberjack. Some tarpon resident the year round. Migratory tarpon March, April, May, early June.

Gulf Stream: sailfish, wahoo, dolphin, white marlin.

Regular Catches

From shorelines, bridges, ramps, reefs accessible by skiffs, wading flats: barracuda, bonefish, the groupers, grunts, crevalle jack, jewfish, ladyfish, Spanish mackerel, cero mackerel, muttonfish, permit, redfish, snook, seatrout, mangrove snapper, yellowtail, tarpon.

Offshore, Reef, Gulf Stream: amberjack, false albacore, barracuda, bonito, dolphin, the groupers, kingfish, mackerel, manta, white marlin, sailfish, mako shark, Allison tuna, wahoo.

If you go by charterboat to the Marquesas and Dry Tortugas you will find:

Outstanding

Heaviest concentations of large barracuda, oversize snapper. Wide range of reef and bottom fish. Permit and bonefish at the Marquesas. Wahoo on reefs off the Marquesas.

Best periods for some principal fish

Bonefish—late April, May, June—good the year round. *Barracuda*—year-round. *Snook*—entire year, greatest frequency late spring through fall. *Crevalle jack*—year-round, late spring. *Reef and bottom fish* — year-round. *Permit*—May, June, early July. Year-round. *Tarpon* — some year-round residents. Heavy migrations of larger fish begin in late February, continue through June. *Sailfish*—November, December—taken year-round.

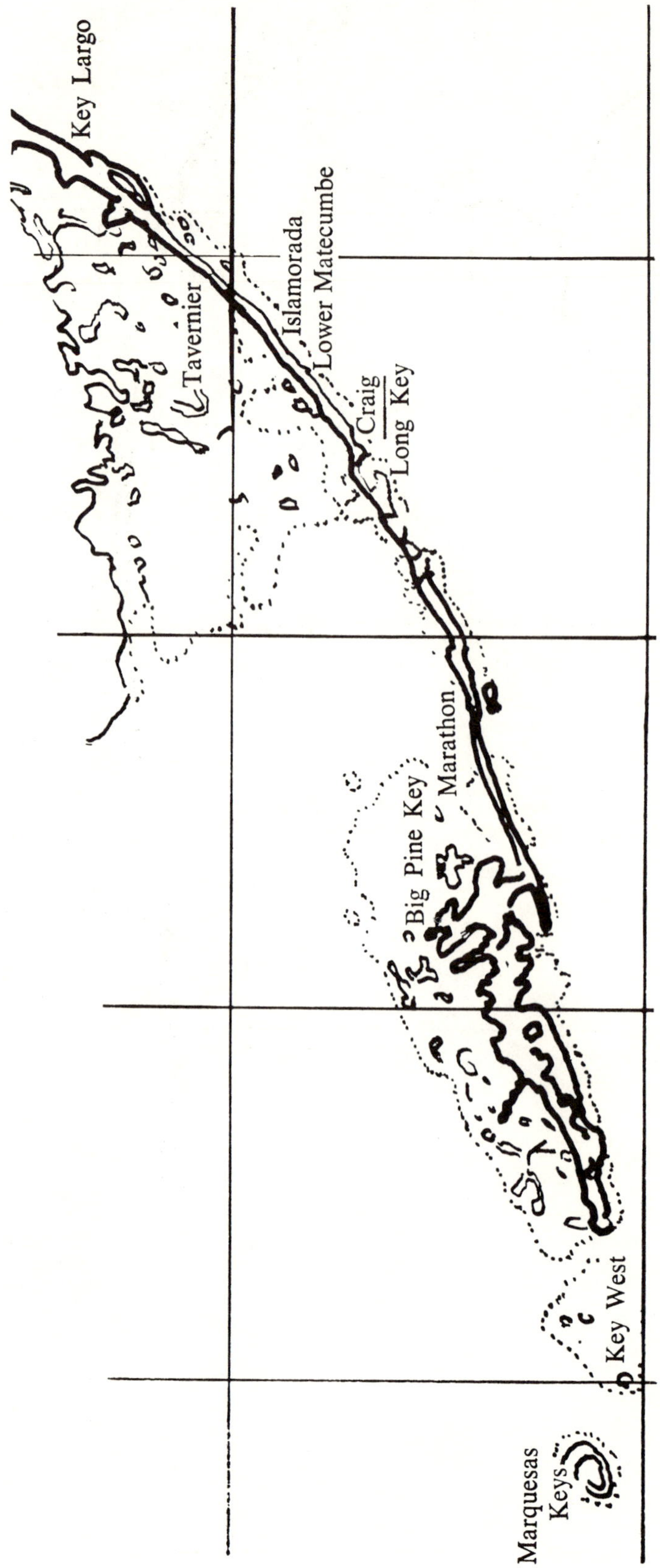

Salt-Water Fishing Areas

Section Five

Florida Bay, Keys' "Backcountry' Lower Everglades National Park Area:

Florida Bay, Flamingo, Cape Sable, Shark River, Lostman's River. A little-fished last frontier of fish-filled waters. Reached by charterboat from centers such as Tavernier, Islamorada, Marathon or from Everglades City. There are innumerable keys, flats and channels in the lower tip of the Everglades. Flamingo offers supplies in this wilderess of waters.

Outstanding

Light-tackle casting for bonefish, redfish, snook, tarpon, permit, seatrout, crevalle jack.

Regular Catches

Tarpon, bonefish, redfish, snook, the snappers, crevalle jack, barracuda, grouper, seatrouts, grunts, jewfish.

Best periods for some principal fish

Tarpon—smaller specimens, year-round. Larger fish, March through September. *Snook*—entire year, spring and summer best. *Crevalle jack*—year-round, January, February exceptional. *Seatrout* — spring months. *Redfish* — spring and summer. Good catches year-round. *Bonefish* (Florida Bay)—spring and early summer. *Jewfish*—year-round.

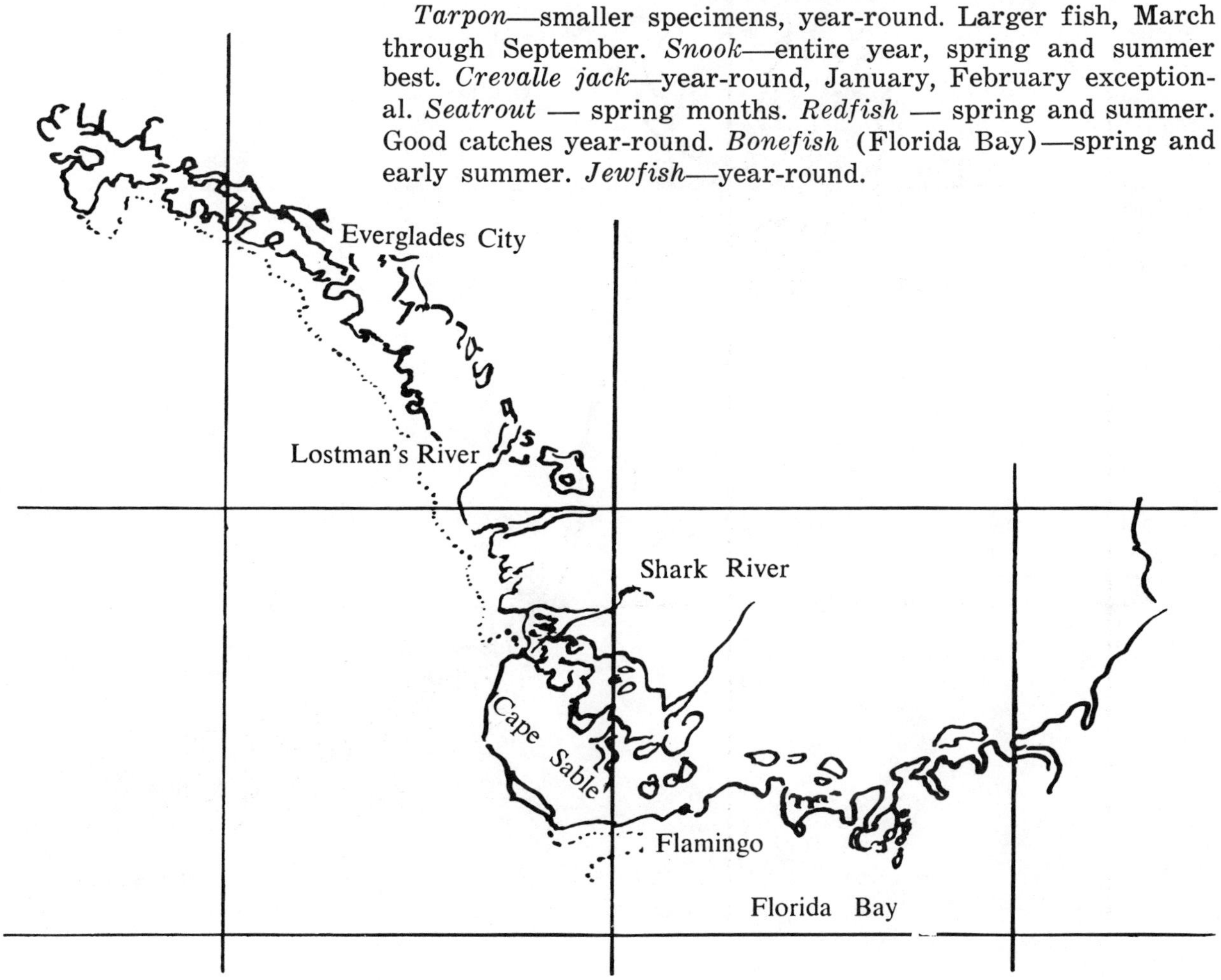

Salt-Water Fishing Areas

Section Six

Lower Gulf Coast

Everglades City, Ten Thousand Islands to Fort Myers

Everglades, Ten Thousand Islands, Marco, Naples, Fort Myers, Caloosahatchee River, Sanibel Island, Captiva Island. (Lower portions of this area are mostly wilderness waters where guides and charterboats are essential).

Outstanding

*Lower portion*s Light-tackle fishing for tarpon, some year round snook, redfish, crevalle jack, small jewfish.

Marco area—snook, pompano along beaches, redfish, tarpon.

Naples to Fort Myers—shoreline fishing for snook, seatrout, redfish, ladyfish—mackerel and blues during runs.

Caloosahatchee River area—big tarpon during migrations, small, year-round.

Offshore: kingfish, groupers, regular bottom species.

Regular Catches

Tarpon, snook, redfish, pompano, mackerel, seatrout, jewfish, crevalle jack, small makos, snappers, kingfish, sheepshead, regular reef and bottom species.

Best periods for some principal fish

Tarpon — smaller specimens year-round in backwaters, rivers, heavy concentrations of larger fish March through September. *Snook*—all year, late summer, early fall outstanding. *Pompano*—late spring, summer. *Seatrout*—all year, heavy runs, spring and fall. *Kingfish*—March, April, late October, November. *Spanish mackerel*—spring, September, early October. *Bluefish*—late March, April, May—November.

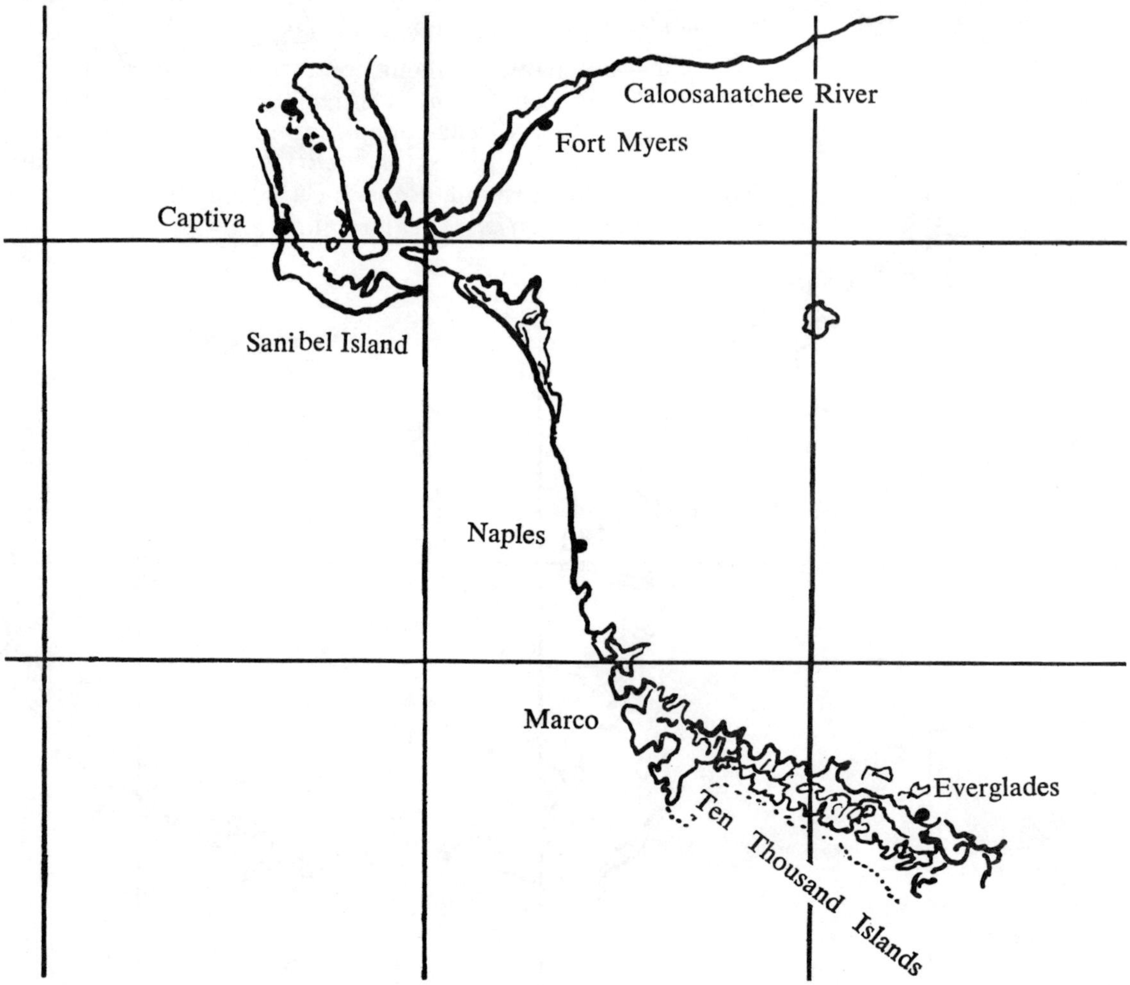

Salt-Water Fishing Areas

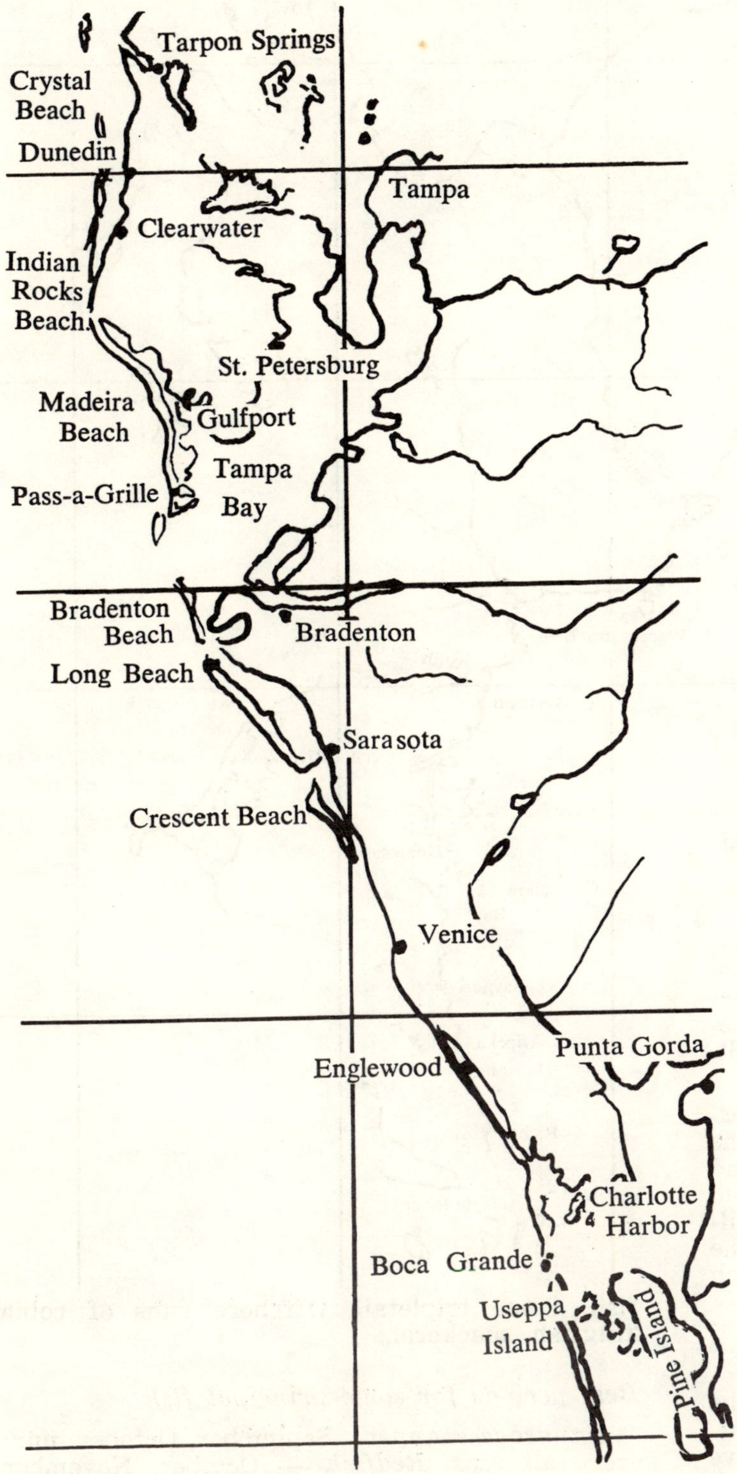

Section Seven

Middle Gulf Coast

Pine Isalnd to Tarpon Springs

South to north

Pine Island, Useppa Island, Boca Grande, Charlotte Harbor, Punta Gorda, Englewood, Venice, Crescent Beach, Sarasota, Long Beach, Bradenton Beach, Bradenton, Tampa Bay, St. Petersburg, Tampa, Pass-a-Grille, Gulfport, Madeira Beach, Indian Rocks Beach, Clearwater, Clearwater Beach, Dunedin, Crystal Beach, Tarpon Springs.

Outstanding

Boca Grande, Useppa Island, Punta Gorda area for tarpon, famed for record sizes and frequencies. Tarpon over entire area from late spring through October, Snook, redfish, seatrout, cobia, kingfish, mackerel, bluefish during runs.

Regular Catches

Tarpon, snook, redfish, mackerel, sheepshead, blues, flounder, grouper, ladyfish, pompano, seatrout.

Offshore: reef fish, amberjack, grouper, regular bottom fish. Kings, mackerel, blues, during runs, some all year, bonito, cobia, jewish, crevalle jack.

Best periods for some principal fish

Tarpon—March, April, May, June, July. All year in rivers, bays. *Snook* — spring through September, good all year. *Bonito*—November. *Redfish*—all year, summer outstanding. *Seatrout* — all year, April, May, October, November outstanding. *Pompano*—late spring through the summer. *Kingfish*—March, April, late October, November. *Bottom and reef fish*—all year. *Spanish Mackerel*—late spring, early fall. *Cobia*—some all year, heavy runs in late March, early April.

Salt-Water Fishing Areas

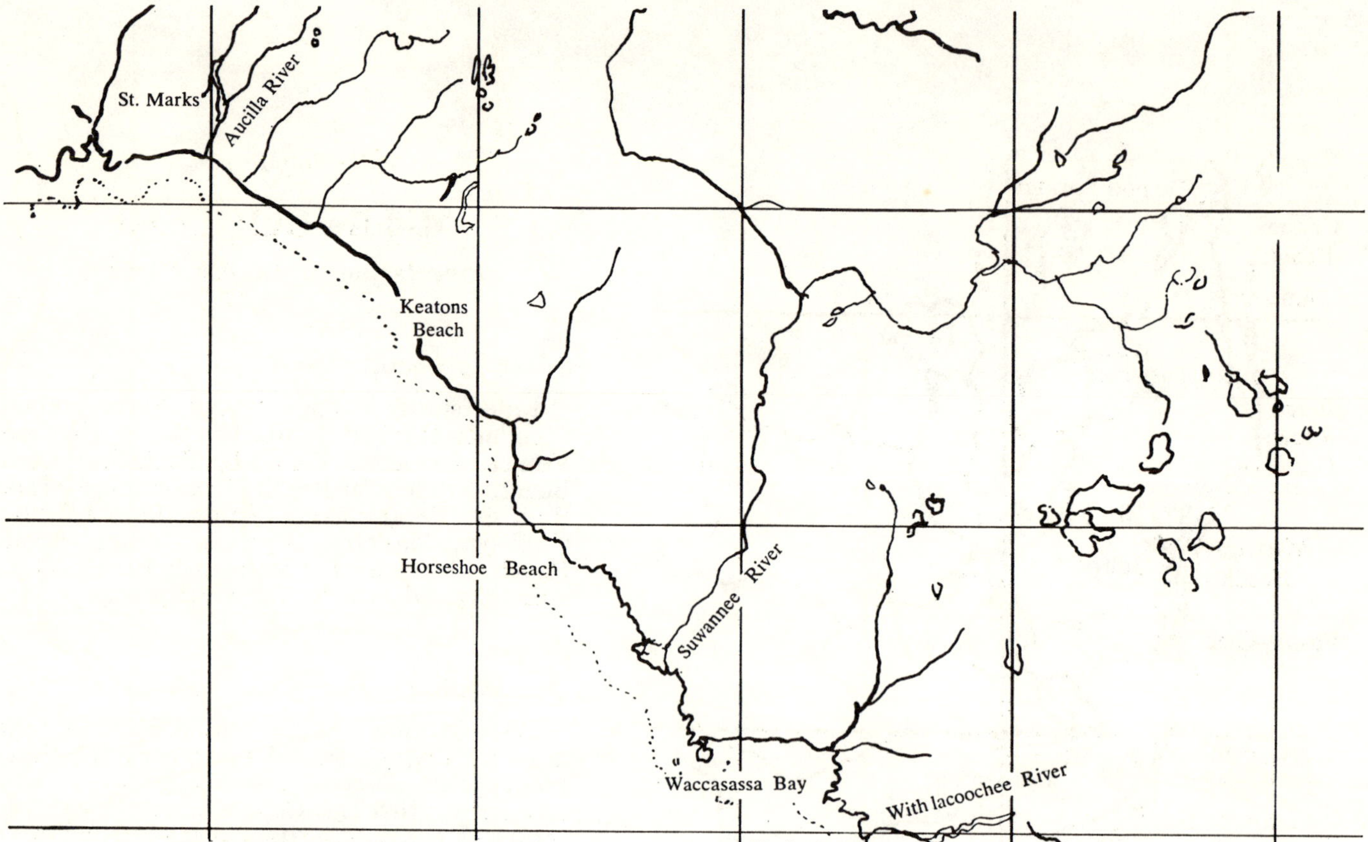

Section Eight

Upper Gulf Coast

Anclote River (Tarpon Springs) to St. Marks

South to north

Anclote River, Port Richey, Hudson, Aripeka, Bayport, Pine Island, Chassahowitska, Homosassa, Crystal River, Withlacoochee River, Yankeetown, Waccasassa Bay, Suwannee River, Horseshoe Beach, Keatons Beach, Aucilla River, St. Marks.

(Much of this area in the more northerly portion is inaccessible because of sparse roads to the coast, shallow coastal waters and marshes, and is hence wild, unspoiled and far from over-fished. Good accommodations, guides, boats, are available at the towns named above. Many of the rivers are famed for brackish water in which salt- and fresh-water species mingle.)

Outstanding

Seatrout, redfish, snook, especially at mouths of rivers. Flounder along beaches. Grouper, bottom fish offshore. Tarpon in summer. Mangrove snapper in all months. Heavy smaller redfish migration in fall months.

Regular Catches

Mangrove snapper, grouper, snook, redfish, tarpon, seatrout, sheepshead, flounder, bottom

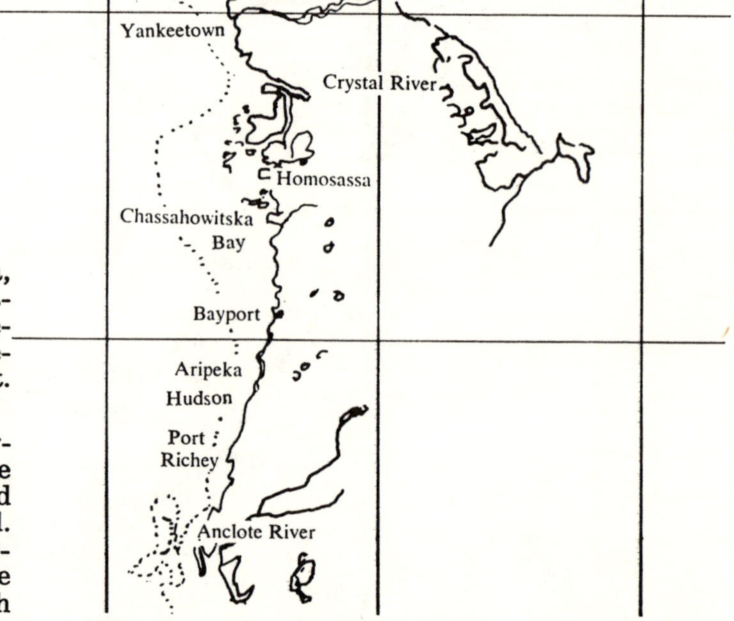

fish. Some tripletail. Offshore runs of cobia, kingfish, mackerel.

Best periods for some principal fish

Mangrove snapper—September, October, numerous all year. *Redfish* — October, November, early December, good all year. *Flounder*—summer months. *Kingfish*—March, April, October, November. *Groupers*—all year. *Snook* — April, May, June, good all year. *Tarpon*—late spring through summer. *Seatrout*—all year, heavy concentrations in late spring, fall.

Salt-Water Fishing Areas

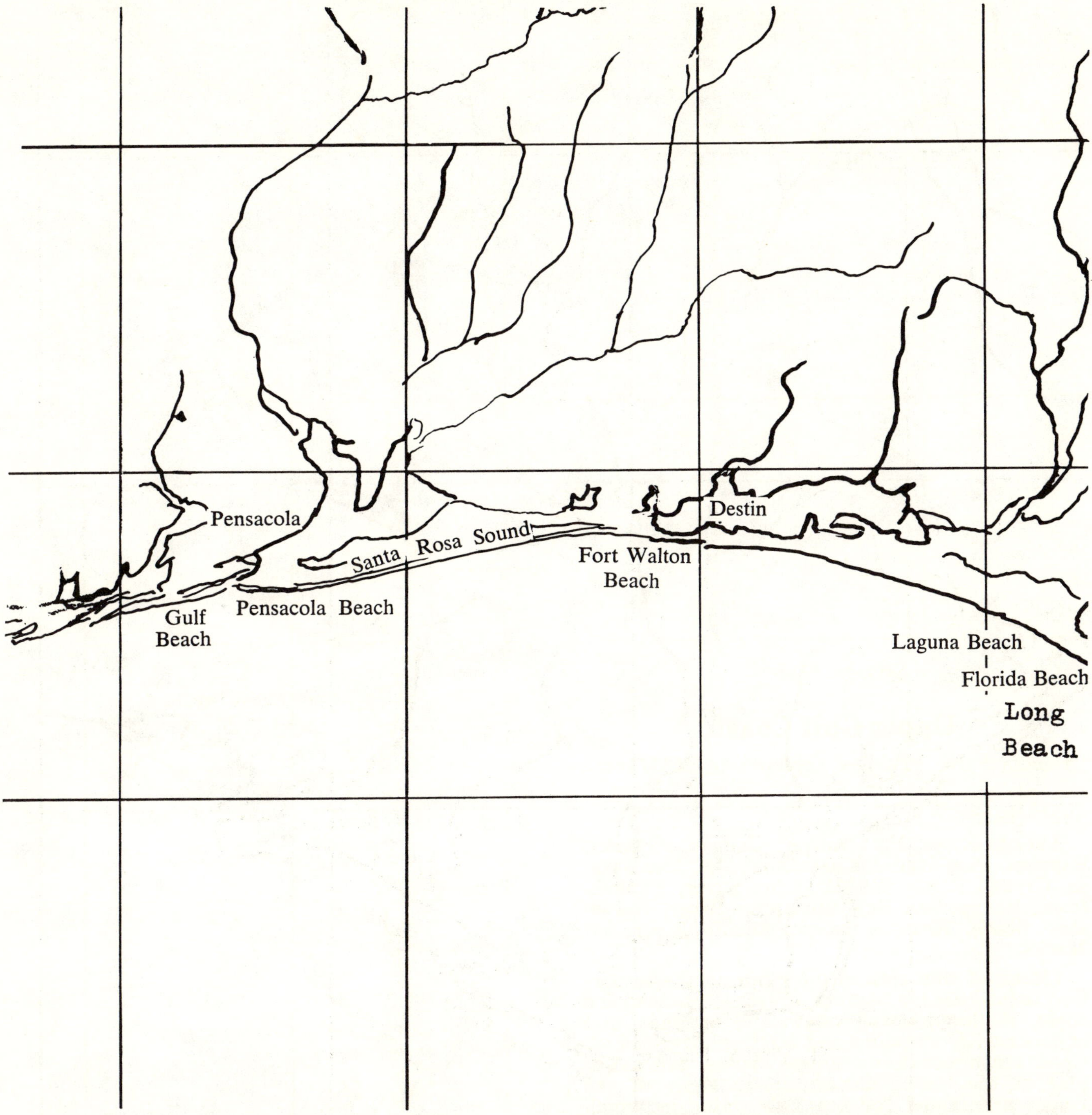

Section Nine

Northwest Gulf Coast

St. Marks to Gulf Beach

East to west

St. Marks, Wakulla Beach, Spring Creek, Panacea, St. Teresa, Lanark, Carabelle, Green Point, East Point, Apalachicola, St. George Island, St. Vincent Island, McNeils, Cape San Blas, Port St. Joe, Beacon Hill, Mexico Beach, Panama City, Long Beach, Florida Beach, Laguna Beach, Destin, Fort Walton Beach, Santa Rosa Sound, Pensacola Beach, Pensacola, Gulf Beach.

Outstanding

Red snapper at offshore banks, Destin, Fort Walton, Pensacola area especially noted. Flounders along beaches.

Offshore—kingfish, Warsaw grouper, regular bottom fish. Record cobia taken during runs.

Salt-Water Fishing Areas

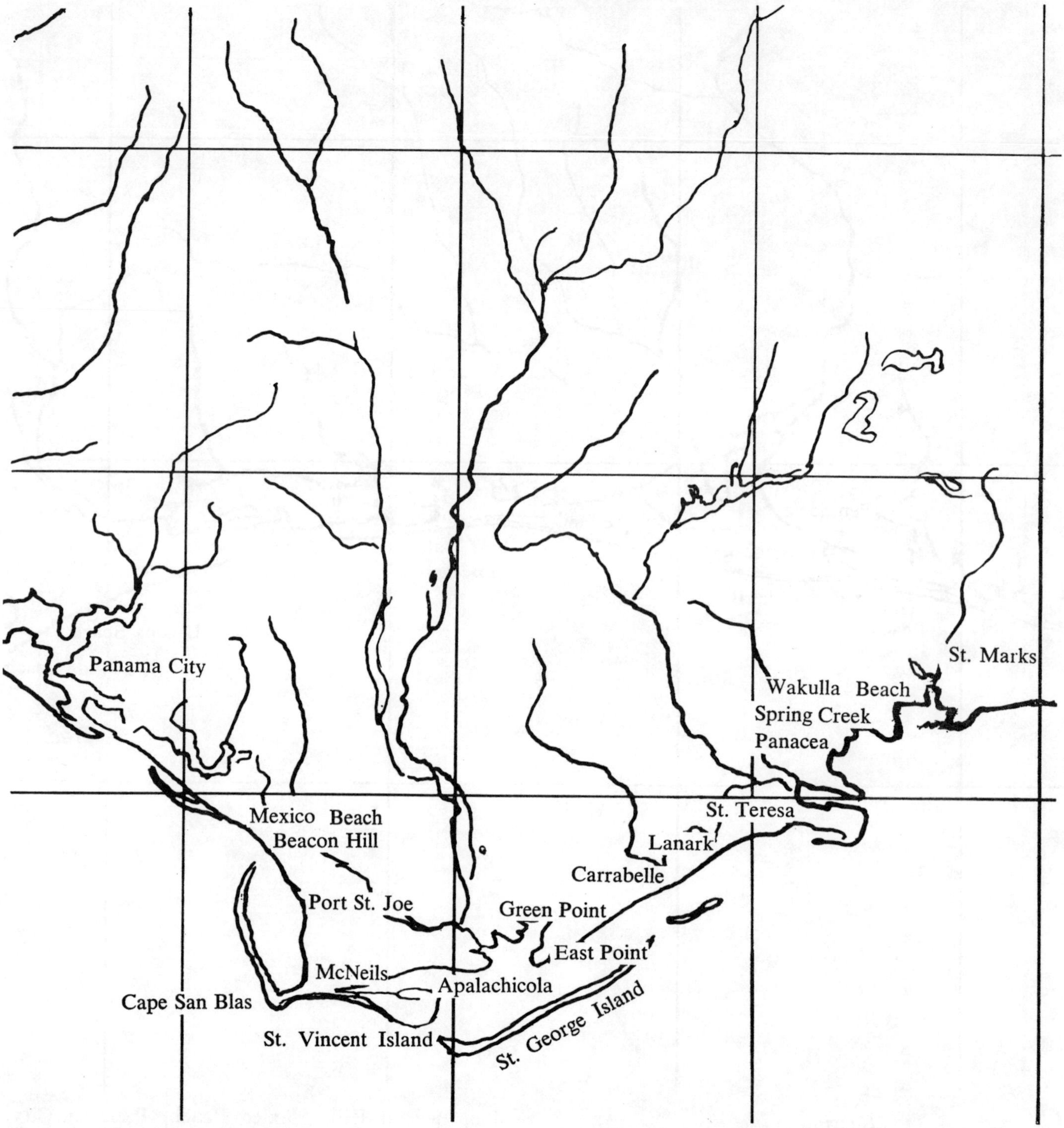

Smaller seatrout on grassy flats. Sheepshead entire area.

Regular Catches

Red snapper, cobia, flounder, seatrout, redfish, kingfish, whiting, Warsaw grouper, blue runners, sheepshead, tarpon, pompano, jewfish, bottom fish.

(An area of beach, pier and small skiff-fishing in bays, backwaters. Seasonal considerations important; winter months liable to be cool, less productive for many species.)

Best periods for some principal fish

Red snapper—all year, fall, winter outstanding. *Cobia*—spring exceptional. *Seatrout*—entire year, fall and early spring best. *Kingfish*—April, May, June. *Snook*—spring, all summer. *Flounder*—fall, early winter. *Tarpon*—late spring, summer.

Fresh-Water Fishing Areas

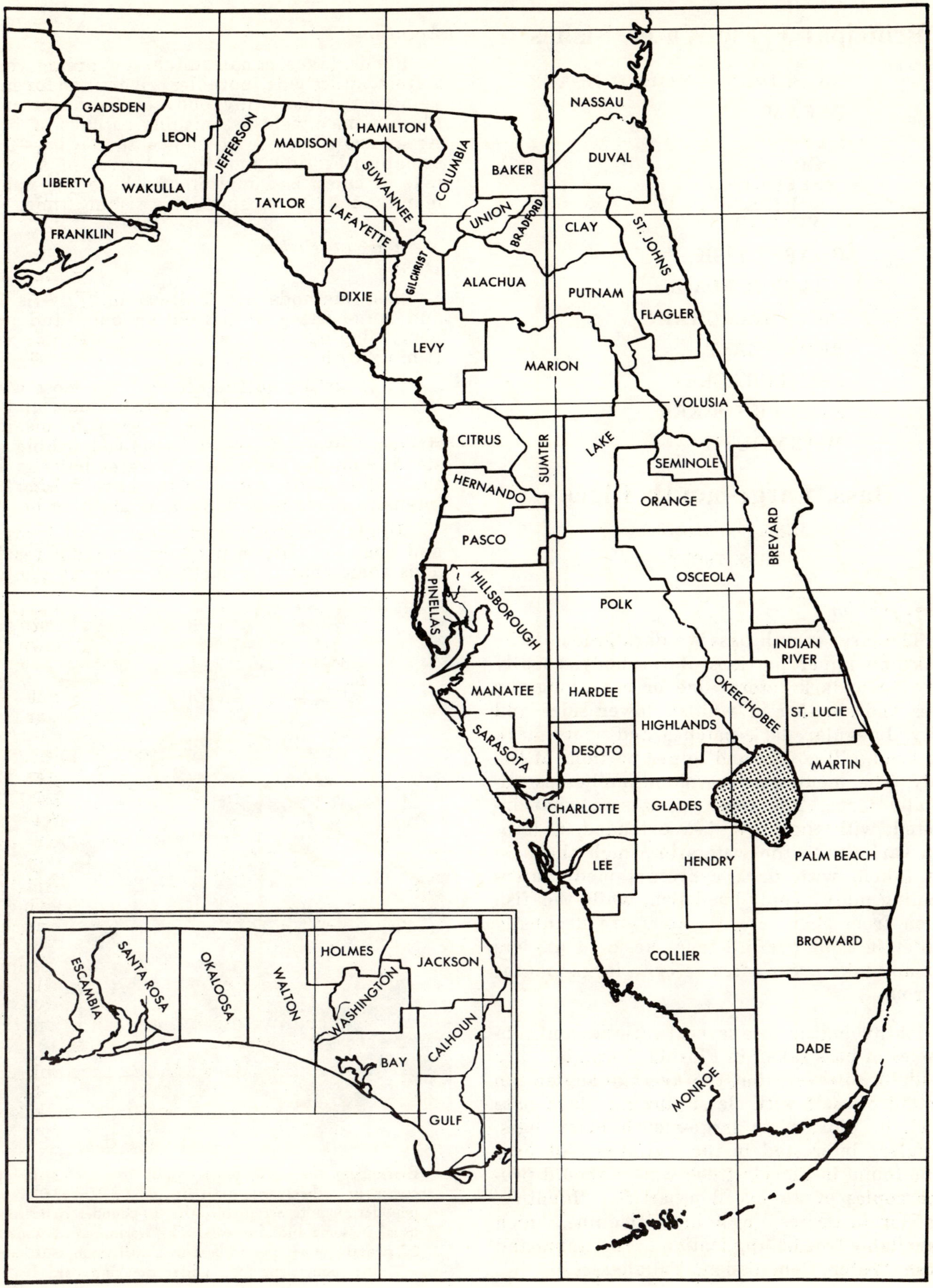

Fresh-Water Fishes

Principal Fresh-Water Fishes

BASS, LARGE-MOUTH BLACK

BREAM

CATFISH,
CHANNEL
SPECKLED
WHITE
YELLOW

COARSE FISH

CRAPPIE, BLACK

PICKEREL, CHAIN

RED-BREAST

SHELLCRACKER

STUMPKNOCKER

WARMOUTH

Bass, Large-mouth Black

Micropterus salmoides

BASS, TROUT

Identification

The large-mouth bass is a dark green on the back and upper portions of the body, usually showing a dark lateral line or bar along the sides and shading to whitish lower sides and belly. Irregular dark patches and spots mark the head, gill covers and upper portions of the body. The mouth, as the name implies, is unusually large. The forehead is somewhat indented, with the lower jaw extended. Coloration varies with the waters in which the bass are taken, with dark cypress-stained waters yielding more deeply-hued fish, while the fish taken from open, clear waters are decidedly lighter in their over-all tone. Resident anglers in many lake areas often refer to large-mouths as trout.

Ichthyologists note several varieties and subspecies of bass taken in Florida. Variations are so slight however, that the average angler can content himself with classifying all black bass taken in Florida as large-mouth black bass. (Anglers interested in the variations of bass to be found in Florida fresh waters should procure copies of an excellent article, "Identifying Florida Basses," by John F. Dequine, which is available free on application to the Game and Fresh Water Commission, Tallahassee.)

Location

Ponds, lakes, canals, ditches, cypress swamp waters, grassbeds, potholes, rivers and streams —in fact, almost any body of fresh water in Florida may yield astonishing catches of bass. Areas are a matter of choice to the bass-fisherman in Florida, and the selection of a town, lake or camp is a matter of where the fisherman would like to spend his fishing time.

Methods of Fishing, Habits

Best methods are bait-casting, fly-fishing and spin-casting with floating bugs and poppers; jigging with weighted bucktails; still fishing with large shiners.

Plug-casting outfits are still the most widely-used gear by Florida bass-fishermen, and almost any standard bass plug will produce strikes. However, fly- and spin-rod fishing are steadily on the increase, top-water baits giving the full dramatic action of the bass rushing into intensive surface-striking and fighting.

Jigging bucktails and other small lures on and near the bottom produce excellent results. This somewhat new method probably evolved

Black Bass, the mainstay of Florida fresh-water fishing comes in rather large sizes at times. While a four-pounder is quite acceptable, this 15-pounder is not unusual in some Florida lakes. The world record is over 22 pounds. A ten-pound bass to a fisherman as a rule, is equivalent to a golfer breaking par.

from similar tactics developed by salt-water fishermen. The lure is allowed to sink to the bottom; then a sharp whipping of the rod flicks the lure into sudden motion for a foot or two. Jigging should be tried on days bass are not striking on the surface, on hot days when they have moved to deeper water.

A common expression among Florida locals that bass "feed with the cows" often becomes fact when waters are high. The bass move off into various grasses, often in water not exceeding a couple of feet in depth. Here, weedless lures, pork rinds and pork frogs, worked slowly, will touch off a frothing explosion in the grass.

Canals and sloughs, open patches in lily-pad ponds are especially productive for anglers using spin- or fly-rods with popper-bugs. There are many varieties of poppers, but their handling requires deftness in achieving the popping sound by a careful twitching of the lure; too much noise is frightening to the fish. This applies also to the use of plugs; the cast must be made deftly without any rough thrashing of the water. Intervals of seconds and a fractional delay should be permitted at the instant of the strike before trying to set the hook.

Bass in Florida definitely respond to certain lures in certain areas, refuse the same baits used in the exact fashion in other waters. Anglers fishing new areas should always question local fishermen on the most successful lures and methods for that particular locale.

Long exploded has been the old cry of the northern bass angler that the Florida largemouth bass is sluggish. They hit with a fierce charge, take to the air for a fine leaping and twisting performance and doggedly battle every inch of the way until boated.

Edibility

Controversial. Smaller specimens, especially from clearer waters, considered good to excellent. Larger bass only fair to poor.

Weights

Reliably reported to 30 lbs. Averages: 4-8 lbs. 10-, 12- pounders not unusual.

Bream

Lepomis marcorochirus

BREAM (Pronounced BRIM), BLUEGILL

Identification

This great Florida favorite pan fish is familiar to northern anglers as the "bluegill sunfish." The body is chunky, the color an olive-green on the back, with an orange-red belly and lower sides. Irregular dark bars mark the upper portion of the body. Dark blues show on the cheeks and mouth. There is a black spot at the upper tip of the gill-covers .

Location

Common throughout all Florida fresh waters.

Methods of Fishing,
Habits

The best methods are cane-pole and bobber-fishing with worms, grasshoppers; and with light spin-gear and fly-rods with tiny lures—bucktails, spinners, flies.

"Brim-fishing" has a large and enthusiastic following in Florida, cane-pole fishermen poking into every remote corner where a gleam of water shows through the brush. The bream is a spectacular little fighter, splashing away furiously when aware of being hooked. The usual somnolent surroundings, the deft, tantalizing nibbles and the succulence of the fish in a sizzling pan, create an ardent army of anglers who endorse pursuit of the bream as a fine sport.

Edibility

Excellent.

Weights

Go to a foot in length, 2 lbs. in weight. Average: ⅓ - ½ lb.

Catfish

CATFISH, CHANNEL

CATFISH, SPECKLED

CATFISH, WHITE

CATFISH, YELLOW

Four principal catfishes are found in Florida fresh waters, the channel catfish, the speckled, the white and the yellow. Of the four the channel catfish is the most highly regarded. its flesh exceptionally tasty and becoming increasingly popular with visiting anglers, although long a favorite of local residents.

The channel cat is coffee-brown to bluish above the lateral line, silver-gray below and irregularly dotted the length of the body. The front spine of the dorsal is sharp and piercing.

Catfish in Florida are most widely caught with set- or trot-lines, and by cane-pole fishermen. However, they will take minnows and cut bait fished near the bottom and will respond to small artificials.

Channel and white catfish are found more often in rivers and cleaner waters, the yellow and speckled catfish in all waters.

Weights

The average weight of the channel cat is 2 to 3 pounds, but it has been reported to 25.

Fresh-Water Fishes

Coarse Fish

The coarse, or rough, fish will be noted only briefly here. They will probably be seen by the visiting angler, some may be hooked, but they should be avoided when possible.

The gars are the most notorious and destructive marauders. There are four varieties in Florida fresh waters: the spotted, the short-nosed, the Florida gar and the long-nosed gar. All are similar in appearance and habits, and menace fry and spawning beds of the game fishes. The long-nosed gar grows to a length of six feet, will strike viciously at plugs and live shiners, but is, like all the gars, difficult to hook because of its shallow, bony mouth. Gars should always be killed and removed from the water when caught.

The chub sucker is of some value as food for game fish. The mouth is small and, like that of all suckers, is located on the underside of the head.

Mudfish are occasionally hooked by fresh-water anglers who are bottom-fishing. The fish is repulsive-looking and has no value as game or food.

The golden shiner will become familiar to Florida anglers, as it is extremely popular as a bait fish. They show a dazzling silver-and-gold and are the most desired of all live baits by large-mouth bass-fishermen.

Crappie, Black

Pomoxis nigro-maculatus

SPECKS, SPECKLED PERCH

Identification

Known as "calico bass" and "crappie" in many parts of the nation, Floridians almost universally designate this fish as "specks" or "speckled perch."

The fish is high-bodied like the other sunfishes, is a dark- to a light silvery-green, with a whitish belly and dark to black spots thickly dotting the body and fins.

Location

All Florida fresh waters. They prefer shallow, reedy waters, weed beds.

Methods of Fishing, Habits

Best methods are very light-tackle or cane-pole fishing, with small live minnows; wet flies, small spinners, spoons, fished below the surface.

Specs are eagerly sought by pan-fish enthusiasts and preferred by many to bream. Small minnows are the most effective bait, although worms are also used. Light-tackle users who learn the trick of a twitching jerking retrieve of small artificials obtain satisfying results. They are active, determined little fighters.

Edibility

Excellent.

Weights

Florida average: ½ lb. Reported to 3 lbs.

Pickerel, Chain

Esox niger

PIKE, PICKEREL, JACKFISH

Identification

The mouth is exceptionally large, with a long snout and large teeth. The body is long, a coffee-green on the back, with green and yellow sides and markings over the entire body in an irregular linklike pattern that gives rise to its name "chain pickerel."

Florida State Game Commission experts note two varieties—the chain pickerel and the red-finned pike—designating them as true pike, in contradistinction to the walleye. Differences are slight, however, evidenced chiefly by dark vertical bars and the redish lower fins on the red-fin pike. The general body shape and coloration of the red-fin and chain pickerel are the same.

Location

Found in shallows and grass of the deeper lakes and streams. It is infrequent in comparison to the large-mouth bass.

Methods of Fishing, Habits

Best methods are those used for large-mouth bass. Usually taken incidentally by bass-fishermen.

The pickerel is a voracious feeder on smaller fish and minnows. Although a hard striker, its fighting qualities and staying power are often somewhat unjustly deprecated by bass-fishermen.

Edibility

Good, the red-fin preferred.

Weights

Average: 2 lbs. Reported to 7 lbs.

Fresh-Water Fishes

Shellcracker

Lepomis microlophus

SHELLCRACKER, RED-EAR

The name is evolved from the fish's habit of cracking the shells of snails and other crustaceans. A bright orange-red patch on the lower gill-covers brings the common designation from fishermen of "red-ear." The breast is yellow.

Shellcrackers are found in clearer fresh waters and streams. They are chiefly fished with worms. The flesh is good, but inasmuch as the shellcracker is one of the smallest of the sunfishes, other pan fish receive more attention from anglers.

Shellcrackers are the delight of the fresh-water cane-pole fisherman. They usually run in uniform size in schools, at about one pound. Sometimes lucky fisherman such as pictured above, get a string with an average of a pound and a half. They are delicious panfish.

Red-Breast

Lepomis auritus

This is the most colorful of the Florida sunfishes, is fished in the same fashion as bream. It will take small artificials and shows a definite preference for streams and swift-moving waters of rivers. The scales of the red-breast have a bluish cast marked with red, the gill-covers are black. Flesh is good. Weights go from $\frac{1}{4}$ lb. - 1 lb.

Stumpknocker

Lepomis punctatus

BLACK-SPOTTED SUNFISH

Identification

Similar in color to the bream, the stumpknocker is marked its entire length with rows of dark-copper dots. The ventral fin is black-tipped.

Location

Most Florida waters, in flowing rivers and streams. In quiet ponds and lakes and in swamp waters they are found feeding at the base of cypress stumps. They do not frequent the larger, muddy, slow-flowing rivers.

Methods of Fishing, Habits

Follow those used for bream. Fishing close to stumps and roots will be rewarding, stumpknockers feeding on snails and other crustaceans.

Edibility

Excellent.

Weights

One-quarter to 1 lb.

Warmouth

Chaenobrythus coronarius

WARMOUTH BASS, GOGGLE-EYE

The Florida goggle-eye, or warmouth, is similar to northern rock bass. They show a strong preference to slow, muddy, quiet waters and feed in heavy grasses and around the base of trees.

Warmouths show a dark-green cast on the back and upper body, have a yellowish belly and are marked with irregular, dark spots on the scales.

They prefer the smallest live minnows, will take smallest artificials. The flesh is good.

Florida's Fresh Waters

Florida offers a vast network of fresh-water lakes, rivers, streams and canals, rich with the great Florida large-mouth black bass, bream and other highly regarded pan fish. It is a common phrase that there are 30,000 named lakes in Florida, a seemingly endless parade of fresh waters, ranging from lakes covering thousands of acres to tiny cypress- or pine-rimmed ponds.

One of the easiest ways to start a hot dispute among Florida fishermen—second only to questioning whether Florida's large-mouth bass are the biggest in the nation—is to select some spot in the central or northern interior portion of the state and declare it to have the finest bass-fishing in Florida. Up will rise a legion of anglers who will stoutly name a dozen lakes or streams they consider to offer far finer fishing. Many towns and fish camps display signboards large and small: 'Bass Capital of the State," or "Bass Capital of the World." local anglers responsible for these signs are sincere in their belief they are telling the truth and will hasten to rattle off figures and tales to back up their assertions. In the summing-up, all the disputants could be more or less justly declared winners, so numerous are the fish populations in so many areas of the state.

An excellent and informative publication issued by the State Conservation Commission on Florida fresh-water fish, records the amazing facts that for each fresh-water license issued in a single recent year, 78.1 pounds of bass were taken; that throughout the state, the year's recorded total—not including the undetermined quantities caught by cane-pole and unlicensed fishermen — accumulated to some 25,000,000 pounds of bass.

What is important for the fresh-water fisherman to know about Florida is that wherever fresh waters are found, whether in the intricate network of lakes that lace the interior of the state, the huge expanse of Lake Okeechobee—the second largest body of fresh water in the nation wholly within its boundaries—or a lily-padded slough of brush water at the side of the road, it is not an unusual feat to step from one's car and tie into good game fish. Many a fine large-mouth bass has been taken from some tiny drainage canal. No ditch or somnolent pond is lightly passed over by the knowing Florida bass-angler, the unexpected becoming the expected from the most unprepossessing patches of water .

Considering the width of the peninsula, it is difficult for the angler in Florida to place himself at any point in the state where he will be more than some 75 miles from salt-water fishing. Thus, if after some days spent in the interior, scoring well with bass and bream, at, say, Lake Tohopekaliga and Alligator Lake near Kissimmee, one wants a change of pace, the good salt-water centers of Melbourne on the Atlantic and the Tampa Bay area on the Gulf are each within a couple of hours' drive.

Conversely, the fisherman moving along Florida's coastlines and wanting to reach productive fresh waters finds himself within easy distance—from a 15-minute run in some instances, to an hour or two—of splendid fresh-water fishing. Thus, as examples, salt-water fishermen at Cocoa who wish to vary their fishing are but a few minutes from magnificent black-bass country at Lake Poinsett and the upper St. Johns River. Similarly, straight across the state at Tarpon Springs, after a few days spent battling with snook, redfish and grouper, a 20-minute drive to Lake Tarpon reveals a fine stretch of bass water, with excellent camps to supply all the angler's needs.

Lakes, river, ponds and streams are listed according to the county, the county seat following the name of the county for a quick identification of the area. In each listing the angler may be assurred of accommodations—boats, tackle, bait, refreshments, cabins, and, of the greatest importance, sound advice from camp-owners, on local conditions, the best lures, special methods and the most likely spots. The fresh-water guides and camp-owners, like those of the salt-water centers of Florida, enthusiastic fishermen themselves, are genuinely interested in seeing that their clients get fish and generous in contributing advice that will help them to do so.

In the matter of camps, accommodations, lodgings, boats and guides, it can be noted that what once passed for a fishing camp, with rather crude, limited accommodations, hardly exists to day in Florida.

For the most part, the visiting angler is sure to find good to deluxe accommodations, with many of the camps boasting air-conditioned cabins. Practically all are equipped with housekeeping facilities and attendant conveniences and luxuries that help to make the off-fishing hours also part of a pleasant vacation.

With the vast increase in the number of women anglers, it is not unusual to see a party of women fishermen pile out of a car with an impressive array of tackle—all set for a weekend's or a week's fishing. Keen competition, tight state regulations and the pride most owners of fishing camps take in their property, have brought about an all-out endeavor by camp operators to meet the requirements of these recent newcomers to the lakes and blue waters. Women who respond to the thrill of the cast and the excitement of a plunging strike no longer have to give much thought to where they will find good or acceptable accommodations in Florida. They choose the waters they want to fish, determine the costs and correctly assume all the expected conveniences will be awaiting them.

The widely-heralded International Women's Fishing Association, which has accomplished much of value since its formation a little over eight years ago, now fishes every portion of the state in small groups or for tournament competition. These highly-skilled anglers fish both the fresh- and salt-water areas of Florida, and their tournaments range from sailfishing contests at the Palm Beaches to the bonefish competition on the Florida Keys in the Islamorada area.

As a special service for all fishermen the state has now set up central information bureaus from which desired information may be obtained in advance. Interested prospective anglers should write directly to the Chamber of Commerce in the town closest to the area selected for fishing, or to central bureaus of the Florida State Chamber of Commerce, Hildebrandt Building, Jacksonville, Florida. Communications can also be directed to the Florida State Game and Fresh Water Commission. Tallahassee, Florida. Replies to these inquiries are prompt and the detailed information provided is most helpful to the newcomer.

Naturally, the listings of fresh waters by Florida counties is not all-inclusive, the "30,000 lakes" alone being beyond the range of compilation here. They are, however, outstanding, proven waters, and can be approached with the certainty that splendid fresh-water fishing is in store. Further, many are in areas where smaller and less-famed lakes and ponds will be revealed to the inquisitive angler, with the accompaniment of the pleasures of discovery of good out-of-the-way spots.

Fresh-Water Fishing Areas

Fresh-Water Fishing Areas by Counties

INCLUDING THEIR COUNTY SEATS, OUTSTANDING LAKES AND RIVERS.

ALACHUA COUNTY—County seat: Gainesville. Fishing waters — Lake Orange, Lake Lochloosa, Newnan's Lake, Santa Fe River, Earleton Beach, Watermelon Pond, Crasco Creek, Santa Fe Lake.

BAY COUNTY—County seat: Panama City. Fishing waters — Pinelog Creek, Bayou George, Martin Bayou, Bear Creek, Sand Lake, River Lake.

BRADFORD COUNTY—County seat: Starke. Fishing waters—Lake Sampson, New River.

BREVARD COUNTY—County seat: Titusville. Fishing waters—St. Johns River, Sand Flats, Lake Washington, Lake Poinsett, South Forty Canal.

BROWARD COUNTY—County seat: Ft. Lauderdale. Fishing waters—Miami Canal. Everglades, Sinew River Canal.

CALHOUN COUNTY—County seat: Blountstown. Fishing waters — Dead Lakes, Upper Dead Lakes, Chipola River, Apalachicola River.

CITRUS COUNTY — County seat: Inverness. Fishing waters—Lake Tsala Apopka, Withlacoochee River, Crystal River, Chassahowitzka River, Homosassa River, Lake Bradley.

CLAY COUNTY — County seat: Green Cove Springs. Fishing waters—Peter's Creek, Doctors' Lake, St. Johns River, Lake Geneva, Smith Lake, Hall Lake, Black Creek, Kingsley Lake, Doctors' Inlet.

COLLIER COUNTY—County seat: Everglades. Fishing waters—Lake Trafford.

COLUMBIA COUNTY — County seat: Lake City. Fishing waters—Sandy Pond, Ogden Lake, Santa Fe River.

DADE COUNTY—County seat: Miami. Fishing waters — Tamiami Trail Canal, Miami River.

DIXIE COUNTY — County seat: Cross City: Fishing waters—Suwannee River.

DUVAL COUNTY—County seat: Jacksonville. Fishing waters — Julington Creek, Cedar River, Goodby Lake, St. Johns River, Davis Creek, Ortega River, Trout River, Big Pittsburgh Creek.

ESCAMBIA COUNTY — County seat: Pensacola. Fishing waters—Escambia River, Perdido River.

FLAGLER COUNTY — County seat: Bunnell. Fishing waters—Lake Diston.

FRANKLIN COUNTY—County seat: Apalachicola. Fishing waters — Apalachicola River, Huckleberry Creek, Crooked River, Ochlockonee River.

GADSDEN COUNTY — County seat: Quincy. Fishing waters—Lake Talquin.

GICHRIST COUNTY—County seat: Trenton. Fishing waters — Suwannee River, Santa Fe River.

GLADES COUNTY—County seat: Moore Haven. Fishing waters—Lake Okeechobee, Kissimmee River, Caloosahatchee River.

Fresh-Water Fishing Areas

GULF COUNTY—County seat: Wewahitchka. Fishing waters—Brothers' River, Dead Lakes, Chipola River, Lake Wimico.

HAMILTON COUNTY—County seat: Jasper. Fishing waters—Withlacoochee River.

HENDRY COUNTY — County seat: Labelle. Fishing waters—Caloosahatchee River.

HERNANDO COUNTY—County seat: Brooksville. Fishing waters—Hunters' Lake, Withlacoochee River, Neff Lake.

HIGHLAND COUNTY—County seat: Sebring. Fishing waters—Arbuckle Creek, Kissimmee River, Bonnet Lake, Tsala Apopka Lake, Istokpoga Lake, Lake June, Lake City, Lake Clay, Lake June-in-Winter, Gator Lake.

HILLSBOROUGH COUNTY — County seat: Tampa. Fishing waters — Little Manatee River, Hillsborough River, Lake Panasoffkee.

HOLMES COUNTY — County seat: Bonifay. Fishing waters—Chocti River, Andrews Lake.

INDIAN RIVER COUNTY—County seat: Vero Beach. Fishing waters—Blue Cypress Lake.

JACKSON COUNTY—County seat: Marianna. Fishing waters — Lake Ocheese, Merritt's Mill Pond, Blue Springs.

JEFFERSON COUNTY—County seat: Monticello. Fishing waters — Lake Miccousukee.

LAKE COUNTY—County seat: Tavares. Fishing waters—Lake Susan, Lake Louise, Haynes Creek, St. Johns River, Lake Eustis, Lake Griffin, Lake Harris, Lake Yale, Dora Canal, Lake Apopka, Apopka Canal, Lake Cherry, Dead Lakes, Lake Indigo, Oklawaha River, Lake Dora, Minihaha, Lake George, Lake Unity.

LEON COUNTY — County seat: Tallahassee. Fishing waters—Lake Talquin, Ochlockonee River, Lake Jackson, Lake Iamonia, Lake Munson, Lake Miccosukee.

LEVY COUNTY—County seat: Bronson. Fishing waters—Withlocoochee River, Stafford's Pond, Suwannee River, Long Pond, Wacasassa River, Wekiva River.

LIBERTY COUNTY — County seat: Bristol. Fishing waters—Florida River, Devil Creek, Equaloxie Creek, Kennedy Creek, River Styx, Ochlockonee River, Duval Creek, Outside Lake, Owl Creek.

MANATEE COUNTY — County seat: Bradenton. Fishing waters—Braden River, Ward Lake.

MARION COUNTY — County seat: Ocala. Fishing waters—Oklawaha River, Lake Weir, Withlacoochee River, Orange Lake, Lochloosa Lake, Halfmoon Lake, Lake Kerr, Little Lake Kerr, Church Lake, Long Lake, Lake Griffin, Lake George, Salt Springs, Lake Eton, Lake Harris, Sunset Harbor, Lake Warner.

MARTIN COUNTY—County seat: Stuart. Fishing waters—South fork of St. Lucie River, North fork of St. Lucie River.

NASSAU COUNTY—County seat: Fernandina Beach. Fishing waters — St. Mary's River, Little St. Marys River.

OKALOOSA COUNTY — County seat: Crestview. Fishing waters—Shaal River, Yellow River.

OKEECHOBEE COUNTY—County seat: Okeechobee. Fishing waters—Lake Okeechobee, Taylor Creek.

ORANGE COUNTY — County seat: Orlando. Fishing waters — Lake Apopka, St. Johns River, Lake Johns, Lake Carlton.

OSCEOLA COUNTY—County seat. Kissimmee. Fishing waters — Lake Marion, West Lake Tohopekaliga, Lake Tohopekaliga, Alligator Lake, Lake Lizzie.

PALM BEACH COUNTY—County seat: West Palm Beach. Fishing waters—Lake Mangania, Lake Osborne, Lake Okeechobee, Everglades.

PASCO COUNTY — County seat: Dade City. Fishing waters—Ester's Lake, Lake Saxon, Lake Gilbert, Lake Pasadena, Keystone Lake.

PINELLAS COUNTY — County seat: Clearwater: Fishing waters—Lake Tarpon, Lake Seminole, Salt Lake.

POLK COUNTY—County seat: Bartow. Fishing waters— Lake Marion, Blue Lake, Kissimmee River, Marion Creek, Lake Howard, Lake Pierce, Lake Shipp, Lake Parkee, Lake Juliana, Lake Ariana, Lake Reedy, Lake Arbuckle, Lake Deer, Clinch Lake, Lake Agnes, Lake Gun.

PUTNAM COUNTY — County seat: Palatka. Fishing waters—St. Johns River, Lake Crescent, Lake George, Oklawaha River.

SEMINOLE COUNTY—County seat: Sanford. Fishing waters—Lake Jesup, Wekiva River, St. Johns River, Lake Monroe, Lake Harney, Lake Puzzle, Lake Brantley.

ST. JOHNS COUNTY—County seat: St. Augustine. Fishing waters—St. Johns River, Julington Creek, Trout Creek, Pellicer Creek, 6-Mile Creek.

SUMTER COUNTY—County seat: Bushnell. Fishing waters—Lake Panasoffkee, Lake Dekon, Withlacoochee River.

VOLUSIA COUNTY — County seat: DeLand. Fishing waters—St. Johns River, Spring G[illegible] den Lake, Lake Beresford, Lake H[illegible]